Empowering Families

The home–school connection is important to student literacy achievement. However, it can be time-consuming to develop and implement programming that keeps families engaged and involved. *Empowering Families* makes it easier to accomplish these goals! Chock-full of step-by-step plans for arranging a variety of parent/caregiver meetings and literacy booster events, the book enables educators to get families involved in their children's learning in ways that are fun and non-intimidating.

By hosting these events at your school, you'll be empowering families to . . .

- read aloud to their children at home;
- minimize the summer slide;
- encourage male involvement in literacy;
- help their children avoid homework hassles;
- and much, much more!

Bonus: The book includes ready-to-use handouts for your events, such as announcement sheets, follow-up evaluations, and tipsheets that describe ways parents can reinforce literacy at home. These handouts are photocopiable and the tipsheets are also available for easy download from our website at www.routledge.com/9781138803114. Spanish versions of the tipsheets are available on our website as well.

Judy Bradbury has taught reading and writing to students from preschool through high school, as well as graduate-level literacy courses. She presents widely at conferences and offers professional development on topics of literacy.

Susan E. Busch has over 25 years of experience as a reading specialist in New York. Now retired from teaching, she continues to present family literacy workshops and offer consulting to school districts.

Empowering Families

Practical Ways to Involve Parents in Boosting Literacy, Grades Pre-K–5

*Judy Bradbury and
Susan E. Busch*

Routledge
Taylor & Francis Group

NEW YORK AND LONDON

First published 2015
by Routledge
711 Third Avenue, New York, NY 10017

and by Routledge
2 Park Square, Milton Park, Abingdon, Oxon, OX14 4RN

Routledge is an imprint of the Taylor & Francis Group, an informa business

Library of Congress Cataloging-in-Publication Data
Bradbury, Judy. Empowering families : practical ways to involve parents in boosting literacy, grades preK-5 /
  Judy Bradbury and Susan Busch.
    pages cm
  Includes bibliographical references and index.
  1. Family literacy programs—United States. 2. Reading (Early childhood)—United States. 3. Reading—
Parent participation—United States. 4. Home and school—United States. I. Busch, Susan. II. Title.
  LC151.B715 2015
  372.42′5—dc23   2014036753

ISBN: 978-1-138-80309-1 (hbk)
ISBN: 978-1-138-80311-4 (pbk)
ISBN: 978-1-315-75391-1 (ebk)

Typeset in Times New Roman
by Apex CoVantage, LLC

ClipArt used with permission from Microsoft

Printed and bound in the United States of America by Publishers Graphics,
LLC on sustainably sourced paper.

Contents

Meet the Authors . . . .*ix*
Acknowledgments. . . . .*xi*

Part I: Introduction

Chapter 1: Empowering Families: Getting Started....................**3**

**Chapter 2: Tips for Conducting Successful Literacy
Booster Meetings and Family Literacy
Events**..**8**

Part II: Staff Development Sessions

Chapter 3: The Power of the Home–School Connection..........**15**
Teacher Resource Packet...25

Part III: Parent/Caregiver Literacy Booster Meeting: Three-Part Series

**Chapter 4: Why Should I Read to My Child (and How,
When, and Where)? Session 1: Getting
Started and Keeping On**..**37**
Session 1 Parent/Caregiver Resource Packet 47

**Chapter 5: Why Should I Read to My Child (and How,
When, and Where)? Session 2: Reading
Aloud to Older Children and Websites of
Interest to Parents, Caregivers, and Kids**...............**56**
Session 2 Parent/Caregiver Resource Packet 63

**Chapter 6: Why Should I Read to My Child (and How,
When, and Where)? Session 3: Reading Here,
There, and Every-Which-Where!**.............................**68**
Session 3 Parent/Caregiver Resource Packet 75

Part IV: Additional Parent/Caregiver Literacy Booster Meetings and Family Literacy Events

Chapter 7: Organize It! And Avoid Homework Hassles...........**87**
Organize It! Parent/Caregiver Resource Packet 96

Chapter 8: **Wrap It Up! Gifts That Entertain and Support Learning**..**106**

Wrap It Up! Parent/Caregiver Resource Packet............................115

Chapter 9: **A Night Out with the Guys . . . and the Kids! Encouraging Male Involvement in Literacy**......**120**

A Night Out with the Guys . . . and the Kids! Parent/ Caregiver Resource Packet...129

Chapter 10: **Celebrating Us! Our Culture and Heritage: Sharing Stories, Food, Traditions, and Goodwill** **139**

Celebrating Us! Teacher Resources...145

Part V: Year-End Parent/Caregiver Literacy Booster Meeting

Chapter 11: **School's Out! Now What? Ideas for Minimizing the "Summer Slide"**.........................**167**

School's Out! Now What? Parent/Caregiver Resource Packet 176

Part VI: Additional Teacher Resources

Chapter 12: **Take-Home TipSheets** **187**

Appendix

Literacy Booster Event Attendance Register...........................**211**

Literacy Booster Event Evaluation Forms **213**

Literacy Booster Meeting Notes..**214**

---

eResources

The Take-Home TipSheets in this book can be downloaded and printed for educational purposes. You can access these downloads by visiting the book product page on our website at www.routledge.com/9781138803114. Then click on the tab that says "eResources," and select the files. They will begin downloading to your computer.

Bonus: Included with the eResources are two extra features not in the book: 1) Spanish versions of the Take-Home TipSheets, and 2) a PowerPoint presentation, "Why Read Aloud to My Child?" that you can use during your Literacy Booster Series.

Meet the Authors

A literacy specialist who has taught students from preschool through college, **Judy Bradbury** is the author of *The Read-Aloud Scaffold: Best Books to Enhance Content Area Curriculum;* the Children's Book Corner series of resource books for teachers, librarians, and parents; and the Christopher Counts! series of picture books for ages 4–7. *Empowering Families: Practical Ways to Involve Parents in Boosting Literacy, Grade Pre-K–5* is Judy's eleventh book. She also writes a monthly column on character education for *LibrarySparks* and contributed regularly to *Children's Writer* and the annual *Writer's Guide.* Judy teaches graduate courses in literacy and writing for children. She is a freelance editor and writing consultant for educational publishers, business organizations, and individuals. An advocate for promoting reading through community initiatives, Judy has received awards from the New York State Reading Association and the Niagara Frontier Reading Council, for which she is the professional development chair.

Judy presents workshops nationally on the topics of literacy and the importance of reading aloud to children. For more information, visit www. judybradbury.com or connect with Judy on LinkedIn.

Susan E. Busch received her BA degree and elementary education certificate from the New York State University College at Brockport in 1974. She received her EdM as a reading specialist from the State University of New York at Buffalo in 1979, where she served as a graduate assistant for four semesters following graduation.

With a career in education spanning 38 years, Mrs. Busch taught in four public school districts and the Catholic Diocese of Buffalo. She received certification from the National Board of Professional Teaching Standards (NBPTS) in early and middle childhood reading and language arts. Susan also completed training as a Ready, Set, Read facilitator for Every Person Influences Children (EPIC).

For the past 18 years, Susan has focused on her passion—the home–school connection—by serving on the Family Literacy Sub-Committee of the District Language Arts Committee in the Ken-Ton School District, researching and developing parent education programs while working full time as a reading teacher. She has conducted over 150 workshops for parents and students and has presented at the district level for the Ken-Ton Staff Development Center. She has presented her family literacy programs to state and local professional organizations.

A member of the International Reading Association, New York State Reading Association, and Niagara Frontier Reading Council (NFRC) for over 20 years, Susan served on the Board of Directors of the NFRC for 16 years and was the outreach chairperson for 13 years. She continues to serve on the Outreach Committee where she coordinates the Habitat for Humanity book basket presentations and assists with the Nicaragua Mission Project.

Mrs. Busch received the Niagara Frontier Reading Council's Service to Reading Award and the New York State Reading Association's (NYSRA) Service to Reading Award in 2000. Promoting collaboration between school children and those serving in the military, Susan received the Veterans of Foreign Wars (VFW) NYS Citizenship Teacher of the Year Award in 2007. Susan was also honored in 2008 by the Town of Tonawanda Youth Board with the Robert Swift Service to Youth Award for her widespread efforts in schools and after-school clubs and for her work with the Civil Air Patrol cadet program. In March 2013, Mrs. Busch was appointed by the National Headquarters of Civil Air Patrol to a character development instructor position in the cadet program.

Having retired from full-time teaching in 2012, Mrs. Busch continues to present workshops to students, parents, and teachers as a family literacy consultant. For more information, visit www.susanebusch.com.

Acknowledgments

The completion of this resource satisfies a desire I have had for several years to offer educators meaningful, creative, and doable ideas for empowering parents and caregivers to impact their children's literacy, academic achievement, and ultimately their success in life. School and home must work together to help our children flourish, and literacy is a vital link. I reached out to Sue to collaborate with me on this book. For two decades I have witnessed her professional expertise, as well as her dedication to seeking ways to boost literacy through creative programming that extends beyond the school day. When I teach students in graduate education programs, I tell them they must have a "fire in their gut" for teaching if they intend to make a difference in children's lives. Sue's got it.

Thanks to accomplished children's author Marsha Hayles, who granted me permission without reservation to share a portion of our workshop for parents in this resource. Marsha's smart, funny, loyal, and a redhead; and I'm lucky to call her a dear friend. Thanks to poet and friend Amy VanDerwater and tech guru Mark Busch for agreeably and patiently sharing some of their estimable knowledge regarding social media with this clueless but willing learner. Finally, enduring gratitude goes to my husband Gene and my daughter Kelsey for their love and support always, and for cheering me on through the process of pulling this project together. They empower me every day. Their willingness to provide advice, a sympathetic ear, computer and technical assistance, a dream work space, and comic relief is part of the reason this book made its deadline. Their belief in the importance of my work makes its publication all the sweeter.

—Judy

Having developed programs for students and their families for many years, it had been my dream to put pen to paper and document my events and programs for others in the field to use. I had no idea where to start or how to complete the process. Judy has been an amazing co-author. She has been gracious and patient—sharing her proficiency in the writing craft, her editing prowess, her professionalism, and her vast knowledge of children's literature. I would never have completed this project without her guidance and friendship.

Special heartfelt thanks to my photographers, Mark Andrew Busch, Steven Truitt, and Kathryn Walker. They all made time in their busy schedules to take the perfect photos needed. It's not always easy photographing kids! My gratitude to Ellen Connell, who translated some of our materials (see eResources) for the benefit of Spanish-speaking families. And, especially, thank you to my son, Mark Busch, who was invaluable in expanding my experience and knowledge of the art and science of computers.

—Sue

Huge, wholehearted thanks go to our editor Lauren Davis, who enthusiastically embraced and supported this project from proposal to bookshelf; editor Alex Masulis, whose interest in our vision got the ball rolling; marketing coordinator Alexa Tarpey; editorial assistants Emily Greenberg and Marlena Sullivan; and all the dedicated professionals at Routledge from book designers to copy editors who worked tirelessly to make our book look so good. What an amazing team! Thank you.

—Judy and Sue

Part I

Introduction

CHAPTER 1

Empowering Families
Getting Started

Improving literacy by strengthening the home–school connection is a powerful initiative with far-reaching effects. Offering a variety of opportunities for parents/caregivers to interact with the professionals who educate their children—with the goal of boosting literacy while building relationships—is a worthwhile endeavor. Yet with ever-expanding responsibilities, it is often difficult for educators to allocate time to adequately plan, organize, and host events beyond the school day. Whether one is scheduling a series of meetings or a single event for parents, caregivers, and families, attention to myriad details is time-consuming and the prospect can be daunting.

This book will help. Three components aim to enable educators to successfully encourage and support parental/caregiver involvement in bolstering literacy and impacting school success: detailed step-by-step suggestions for implementing a range of parent/caregiver **Literacy Booster Meetings** and **Family Literacy Events;** copy-ready **Parent/Caregiver Resource Packets** for event attendees; and a set of engaging, copy-ready single-page **"Sharing Our Secrets" Take-Home TipSheets** intended for parents/caregivers and ideal for stuffing in backpacks. In addition, bonus **eResources**, which include a set of PowerPoint presentations, additional resources for events, and materials in Spanish, are available online. Together these components offer a cohesive, detailed means for empowering families to team with educators to bolster literacy.

Literacy Booster Meetings—Sessions for parents/caregivers aim to impact literacy and strengthen the home–school connection. The focus is nurturing and invigorating commitment to boosting literacy in the home and cultivating communication between home and school. Meetings offer participants a supportive environment in which to develop and expand knowledge, abilities, and interest in impacting literacy. Simple, effective strategies are shared. Periodic meetings support ongoing involvement while deepening educators' understanding of the roles and responsibilities—as well as the challenges—of the adults directly involved in their students' lives.

Family Literacy Events—Parents, caregivers, and children are welcomed to vibrant programs that take place outside of the academic day. Literacy events for families that offer engaging, entertaining opportunities for learning build positive home–school connections.

"Sharing Our Secrets" Take-Home TipSheets—Sending home brief, eye-catching literacy tips on a regular basis reinforces and extends strategies discussed at Literacy Booster Meetings or experienced at Family Literacy Events. The Take-Home TipSheets also offer suggestions for books, websites, and creative ways to boost literacy. Upbeat, accessible, and engaging Take-Home TipSheets keep parents and caregivers thinking about literacy. The TipSheets are available in color and in Spanish in eResources online.

How do the components of this book satisfy educational standards and goals? The Common Core State Standards (CCSS), as well as other educational initiatives, guidelines, and regulations inform and drive education in today's schools. The need for vigorous support from the home to boost literacy has never been greater. Working together, home and school improve students' success in reaching challenging academic goals.

The National PTA has established standards for family-school partnerships. These include welcoming families into the school environment, developing effective communication, and collaborating as equal partners in supporting student learning (see www.pta.org/programs/content.cfm?ItemNumber=3126). The CCSS state:

> The skills and understandings students are expected to demonstrate have wide applicability outside the classroom. . . . In short, students who meet the standards develop the skills in reading, writing, speaking, and listening that are the foundation for any creative and purposeful expression in language. (CCSS Introduction, page 3)

Why strive to strengthen home–school connections? Educators as well as parents/caregivers have much to gain from home–school partnerships. School faculty and staff gain insight into the joys, challenges, needs, and dreams of the parents and caregivers of the students with whom they work. Literacy Booster Meetings, Family Literacy Events, and helpful written communications bridge home and school. Educators become more accessible, and the school environment seems less formidable to parents/caregivers. Adults in children's lives benefit from a variety of opportunities to get to know and appreciate one another and to form alliances that impact student success. Supportive faculty and staff demonstrate how essential parents/caregivers are to their children's achievement of school-related goals. Together, the adults in children's lives become collaborative literacy partners. With a shared mission, they are powerful advocates with viable and achievable goals.

What are parent/caregiver literacy booster meetings? Developing and nurturing solid parenting skills may well be a by-product of the **Literacy Booster Meetings**, but this is not the intended purpose; rather, the goal is boosting literacy skills for the benefit of children while strengthening the home–school dynamic.

Encouraging open discussion is a hallmark of the programs developed for this resource. It is vital that educators and parents/caregivers speak honestly and feel comfortable doing so. Much can be learned from one another. Barriers and negative feelings that may have originated when parents/caregivers were students themselves must be overcome. Encouraging the use of first names, for example, allows parents/caregivers to feel more relaxed and on equal footing with their children's teachers and school staff. In all instances, parents/caregivers should feel respected, supported, and lauded for their commitment to fostering literacy in the home.

The optimal size for Literacy Booster Meetings is approximately 20 participants, with 1–2 leaders. Encourage school support staff, such as social workers, school psychologists, media specialists, and counselors to attend. It's ideal if the principal participates as well.

The length of individual programs is generally 1–2 hours. Each features a variety of activities and includes a 10–15-minute break. A read-aloud is an essential component of Literacy Booster Meetings, as is ample time for discussion. Specific suggestions for what parents/caregivers can do at home to boost literacy are central to each session. The opportunity for parents/caregivers to share their experiences, their triumphs, and their frustrations is also an integral feature of a dynamic Literacy Booster Meeting.

When conducting Literacy Booster Meetings, the emphasis is on demonstrating strategies rather than talking about them. Participants are offered opportunities to try techniques that are introduced. This enables parents/caregivers to experience and prepare for their implementation. Literacy Booster Meetings ought to reflect the learning that takes place in the classroom. Parents/caregivers then have a real sense of what and how their children are learning in the academic setting; this insight supports learning in the home.

Literacy Booster Meetings can be scheduled to take place immediately following the school day or in the early evening. Meetings also can take place during the school day if such scheduling is feasible. It is advisable to keep the time and day consistent for the duration of a series of related sessions. However, varying the time and day for stand-alone meetings over the course of the school year will meet the needs of parents/caregivers with a variety of schedules. Some parents/caregivers may not be able to attend on Wednesday evenings, for example, but are available on Monday afternoons. Creatively schedule to engage parents/caregivers and generate enthusiasm. Consider a lunch meeting, an ice cream social, or attaching a book raffle to the event.

Survey parents/caregivers for preferred meeting times and provide childcare if it is deemed necessary to the success of the program. Childcare ought to include fun activities and creative play reflecting the philosophy of the parent/caregiver programs. If feasible, offer to provide transportation, whether by public means, car pools, or school bus, to enhance attendance.

Choose welcoming, bright rooms for meetings. The school library or an adequately sized conference room works well. Consider varying the location to allow parents/caregivers to become familiar with various settings within the school. Arrange tables to enhance sharing ideas. Round tables encourage discussion; chairs in rows can inhibit interaction.

Multilingual sessions are encouraged when they reflect the diversity of the school community. This reflects respect for the cultures represented in the school community and the aim to develop and support inclusive home–school connections. Select Literacy Booster Meeting materials are available in Spanish in eResources online.

Follow-up sessions reinforce strategies, allow parents/caregivers to discuss setbacks and successes, and build relationships. Meeting summaries serve as reminders. Related TipSheets offer reinforcement and additional ideas. Feedback from evaluations of events is priceless when developing future programs. Communication is crucial to effective programming.

Strengthening the connection between home and school through ongoing programming requires commitment from the entire school community: administration, faculty, staff, parents/caregivers, and students. With personal investment comes a sense of responsibility—and ultimately—empowerment. Enthusiastic parent/caregiver involvement lies at the heart of successful programming.

When initially scheduling Literacy Booster Meetings, it is preferable to personally invite parents/caregivers. A fall Open House or parent-teacher conferences offer ideal opportunities for extending a personal invitation to parents and caregivers. As meetings become familiar and expected events, invitations can simply be sent home.

How Are Literacy Booster Meetings Structured?

Introduction (5–20 minutes)—A warm greeting, a preview of the session's focus (sometimes as a mini-activity), an explanation of session goals, and a read-aloud of a related children's book are features common to all Literacy Booster Meetings. At each event participants must be made to feel comfortable working together with a shared purpose. Stating names and children's names and grade levels is an effective way to warm up the group. Consider asking participants to briefly interview and introduce each other to the group. Ask participants to briefly share news about their children or recall a tip from a previous session that worked well—or didn't. Encourage participation by posing a general question relating to the topic of the meeting. (Examples: What is one thing your child was excited to learn in school this week? What are you an expert at, or would like to learn more about? In your opinion, what makes learning easy or difficult? Recall a favorite school story either from your past or from your child's experiences. What is one thing about our school or your child's classroom that is making a difference in your child's life?)

The **read-aloud**, a staple of the Literacy Booster Meeting, underscores the importance of reading and demonstrates the joy of being read to. Not only does the read-aloud help focus the session's events, it also models effective read-aloud techniques. Read-alouds rekindle or jumpstart interest in children's literature and underscore the vitality and pleasures of a literacy-rich home. It's essential that all participants can see and hear the book as you read aloud. For small groups, it is suitable to stand before the group and perhaps circulate so everyone can enjoy the illustrations as you read the text. For larger groups, consider using a document reader, opaque projector, or other means of making the book pages easily visible to all. Consider purchasing a big book edition, if available. It is crucial that the read-aloud experience be engaging and that the leader models effective read-aloud techniques.

Part I (15–30 minutes)—The goal of each Literacy Booster Meeting is learning and doing. Everyone is encouraged to participate. Group dynamics and problem-solving build a sense of community as well as a sense of self-worth, confidence, and empowerment.

Break (10–15 minutes)—Offering simple, healthy snacks is optional but encouraged. During breaks, leaders and participants have an opportunity to browse books and socialize.

Part II (20–40 minutes)—Parents/caregivers respond to open-ended questions and discuss Part I, exploring ways to apply strategies at home. Small and large group discussions take place. A unifying thread connecting sessions is the home activity. Often, recapping the home activity experience is an excellent way to begin the following session in a series of related meetings.

Wrap-Up (5–15 minutes)—The purpose of the Literacy Booster Meeting is reviewed and what was accomplished is summarized; if the meeting is part of a series, the leader recaps what participants will try out and report on at the next session. A brief overview of the upcoming session is offered. Participants fill out evaluations; leaders thank participants for coming. Session ends promptly, but leaders remain available for brief questions.

CHAPTER 2

Tips for Conducting Successful Literacy Booster Meetings and Family Literacy Events

Positive connections educators make with parents and caregivers strengthen school support at home. Parent/caregiver involvement is vital to the academic success of students, and educators must enlist active, enthusiastic, and ongoing commitment from the home. Most adults want to help their children succeed academically, but sometimes they aren't familiar with or don't possess a clear understanding of effective methods and tools for boosting literacy. **Literacy Booster Meetings** offer an opportunity for everyone to learn, share, discuss, and become more confident with strategies that bolster literacy. A welcoming atmosphere cultivates powerful partnerships between home and school. Relevant programs fill in the gaps and prompt parents/caregivers to view their role in their child's academic endeavors as critical to success. The following approaches aid in the organization and execution of engaging parent/caregiver programs.

Flexibility—Modify as necessary the resources, suggestions, and schedules contained in this book to best meet the needs of the parents/caregivers and students in your setting. Sessions can be lengthened or shortened. To tighten an existing session, review the Talking Points and select those most beneficial to your audience. To extend a session, allow additional time for discussion or add Talking Points reflecting relevant concerns in your school community.

Scheduling—Survey parents/caregivers or confer with the parent organization at your school to gauge optimum times for holding Literacy Booster Meetings. Scheduling sessions a week or two following parent conferences may yield a better turnout. Teachers can personally invite parents/caregivers to attend and have registration information available to distribute. Parents/caregivers who develop positive relationships with educators often are willing to follow suggestions to help their children succeed in school.

Childcare—Parents/caregivers may not attend school meetings because they are unable to arrange childcare. Since Literacy Booster Meetings are intended for adults only, consider providing childcare. Resources for volunteers include scouting programs, high school childcare classes, college childcare or teacher preparation programs, and Youth Engaged in Service (YES). Arrange for a responsible adult to supervise youth volunteers. Equip the room with age-appropriate games, activities, toys, and books. Adhere to district policies for childcare.

Details—Provide a date by which time parents/caregivers must register for events so adequate materials will be available for all attendees. Allow ample time to respond. Plan to have extra materials on hand so unregistered attendees feel welcome. Thank participants for coming. Note that attendance is a clear signal to children that education is a priority in their home.

Begin on Time—Everyone's time is precious. When Literacy Booster Meetings are managed effectively and contain practical ideas that can be implemented easily at home, parents/caregivers are more likely to attend future events.

Take Notes—Parents/caregivers appreciate being heard, and they want school meetings to be productive. Take notes during Literacy Booster Meetings and generate a brief summary, including thoughts and ideas offered during the session. (A colleague or participant can be enlisted to take notes.) Publish and distribute the summary in parent, school, or district newsletters soon after the Literacy Booster Meeting takes place. Once distributed, those in attendance will have a reminder of what they learned and no doubt will be pleased to see their ideas are valued. Those who were unable to attend the meeting also will benefit from the ideas offered in the summary.

Refreshments—Though not necessary, light fare can enhance the atmosphere, making events feel more welcoming. Simple, healthy snacks and beverages can be provided at a reasonable cost. In Literacy Booster Meetings, breaks offer participants an opportunity to interact with one another and form or renew friendships. Often at such times, participants encourage each other to attend future events, exchange ideas, and offer support for putting Literacy Booster Meeting suggestions in place at home. When customizing a session to meet time constraints, endeavor to include time in the schedule to support and enhance parent/caregiver connections.

Read-Aloud—People young and old enjoy being read to. Beginning each session with a read-aloud will provide parents/caregivers with a model for effective read-aloud techniques they can use at home. Enjoying a book together helps build a sense of community, and it is an effective way to introduce a topic or spark discussion—in school and at home. Always practice the read-aloud in advance of the event. In addition, make provisions that ensure the book will be seen and heard by all participants. Consider a document reader, opaque projector, big book edition, or other means to engage large groups. Model effective read-aloud behaviors.

Inform Custodial Staff—Events may require a change in work schedules or progression of duties. When custodial staff assists with an event, send a note of appreciation. If several events are held throughout the year, consider offering a thank-you gift. Fostering goodwill strengthens relationships within the school community.

Introduce faculty and staff at the outset of the Literacy Booster Meeting. Thank volunteers. Send thank you notes following events. Including a small token of appreciation is a thoughtful gesture. People appreciate acknowledgement of their efforts and may be willing to assist with future Literacy Booster Events as a result of your sincere gratitude.

Seek Input—To be effective, Literacy Booster Meetings and Family Literacy Events must be tailored to the needs of the school community. Solicit ideas for topics and themes at parent conferences or via questionnaire. Elicit responses to a list of possible topics on the school website. Request responses by a specified date.

Be Receptive—Literacy happens at home, whether it is oral family history, storytelling, cooking together, or simply conversing with family and friends. Parents/caregivers may use strategies at home that could be useful at school. They attend Literacy Booster Meetings for tips, but teachers learn from parents/caregivers, too. The adults in children's lives have valuable knowledge and insights to share. Encourage Literacy Booster Meeting attendees to discuss what works with their children. Being interested and receptive to their strategies empowers parents/caregivers to remain active partners in boosting literacy.

Seek Funding—The meetings and events outlined in this resource are relatively inexpensive to undertake. Copy-ready Resource Packets are provided. Other materials commonly can be found at most schools. Books can be loaned from the library. To provide new books, games, or other items for events, consider requesting financial assistance from local community organizations, such as Rotary Club, Elks Club, United Way, or Every Person Influences Children (EPIC). Local reading councils, business organizations, community education programs, and colleges and universities may provide funding or grant opportunities. Search "community organizations/associations" online. Title I funding encourages the use of its resources to provide parent involvement programs. Guidelines must be strictly followed (www2.ed.gov/policy/elsec/leg/esea02/pg2.html#sec1118) and included in the district's annual application. For refreshments, consider requesting funds from your school's parent organization. Approach local grocery stores via formal letter at least a month in advance for donations of simple healthy snacks and beverages. Often stores have a monthly budget for supporting non-profit organizations and earmarked funds are quickly distributed. Stipends for meeting planners and facilitators are desirable but may not be feasible. Providing some form of compensation, such as professional hours or additional personal days, could be considered.

Ensuring Parent/Caregiver Buy-In

The best prepared Literacy Booster Meetings and Family Literacy Events ultimately will be ineffective if parents/caregivers choose not to attend. How to get high-percentage participation? Here are six **C's** that a strategic "buy-in" plan should include.

Connect
- **Face Time**—Personal invitations from teachers are most effective. Follow up by sending home flyers or placing an article in newsletters.
- **Get Organized**—Keep your school's parent organization informed and enlist their support. Request assistance with promoting events.
- **Face Time, Part II**—Encourage parents/caregivers to invite peers.
- **Face Time, Part III**—Enlist principals, staff, and support personnel to personally invite parents/caregivers with whom they come in contact. Supply details and flyers.

Communicate
- **Create Buzz**—Advertise! Advertise! Advertise!
- **Reach Out**—Ask colleagues to place events on classroom calendars and include information in classroom newsletters.
- **Widen the Reach**—Publish information in district newsletters and on school and district websites.
- **Attention, Please!** Write concise, detailed press releases for local newspapers and public service announcements on radio stations and local TV stations.
- **Point and Shoot**—Include a photo for all press releases, if possible.
- **Dear Parent**—A classroom lesson in letter writing instructs students while also inviting parents/caregivers to literacy events.
- **Bright Idea!** Print registration forms on colored paper, if possible. The form will be conspicuous and more eye-catching than one on white paper.
- **Did I Mention . . . ?** Deliver daily verbal reminders in an intriguing, creative way to motivate children to want to attend Family Literacy Events. Preview activities that will be showcased at the event to generate interest.
- **Post It**—Advertise events with colorful, inviting posters placed in visible areas.

Convenient
- **Meet Me!** Be creative and all-inclusive when scheduling sessions. Vary days and times. Think outside the juice box. How about a Breakfast Brunch? A Catch Coffee & Cookies meeting prior to school dismissal? A Sundae Monday? A Super Soup Supper? Pizza anytime is sure to draw a crowd! Regardless of theme, strive to arrange for refreshments. Participants may not have time to prepare a family meal prior to an evening event. Light sustenance provides nourishment and encourages social interaction.
- **Child Space**—Provide childcare during parent/caregiver Literacy Booster Meetings and include that information in any marketing tool used. (See Childcare above.)

Concise

- **Time Out**—Be punctual with starting and ending times. Families plan around advertised schedules.
- **Ready, Set, Go!** Materials should be ready and hardware tested prior to the arrival of participants to avoid delays.
- **Go with the Flow**—Keep the session aptly paced. Don't overwhelm participants with too quick a pace or bore them with a slow crawl.
- **I Get It!** Stress important points but avoid redundancy.

Collaborative

- **I Wonder . . .** Encourage participants to ask questions at any time during the session. There are no dumb questions. Keep answers brief. If unable to answer a question, offer to research the answer and publish it in a future communication.
- **I Hear You**—Encourage participants to share ideas and experiences.
- **Got It!** Note participants' suggestions on chart paper or a whiteboard. Publish and distribute a summary. This demonstrates that their ideas are valued.

Celebratory

- **I Know Just What You Mean**—Keep it light. Even complex topics should be approached with warmth and humor, though care should be taken not to laugh at or minimize serious concerns. Facilitators' personal stories add insight and camaraderie. Just keep it concise!
- **Great Job!** Thank participants for making the effort to attend. By attending such events they demonstrate to their children that education and literacy are a priority in their family.
- **Comic Relief**—If a session is engaging and fun, the word will get out and participation at future events will grow.
- **The End**—At the conclusion of each event, provide a simple takeaway. This will encourage the use of the item at home and promote conversation. Bookplates for the Wrap It Up event and child-constructed airplanes for the Night Out with the Guys event are examples of useful, inexpensive, and fun mementoes for Family Literacy Events.

When the event is over and the lights are out, congratulate yourself on a job well done!

Part II

Staff Development Sessions

CHAPTER 3

The Power of the Home–School Connection

Allow what happens in families and communities to inform schooling.
—Moll and Greenberg, 1990

Much research has been dedicated to proving what teachers and administrators know: developing positive communication between the home and the school benefits students in myriad ways. Students gain greater cognitive competence and attain higher achievement scores when families are involved in school events and activities (Fan and Chen 2001; Epstein and Dauber 1991). Children exhibit stronger problem-solving skills and better attendance (Sénéchal et al. 1998; Hindin and Paratore 2007; Sénéchal and Young 2008). Parents/caregivers view teachers and schools in a more positive light (Epstein and Dauber 1991). Districts and schools often provide programs to inform parents/caregivers of resources for solving student issues as well as activities to enrich and extend their children's education. Programs often

- teach parents/caregivers the philosophy of the school system;
- demonstrate effective methods and materials used in school and at home;
- help parents/caregivers promote solid reading habits;
- give guidelines for providing homework assistance;
- help parents/caregivers develop oral reading skills;
- offer advice on parenting topics;
- provide information and resources on timely topics, such as computer safety; and
- suggest ways for parents/caregivers to communicate effectively with the school.

These are important goals, and this set of sessions for educators is a resource for planning and implementing effective programs that nurture the home–school connection. That connection is a two-way street. Teachers may begin the year with a vision of ideal classrooms based on their backgrounds and experiences. Often this schema is a direct reflection of the values they were exposed to in their early school years: a supportive home where they were read to and activities with books were a regular occurrence; a home where help with homework and projects was assumed, and where education was a top priority. Attending college was an expectation, not an exception. When the reality of their students' family life conflicts with such visions, educators must endeavor to understand, accept, and respect their students' home environment and actively support parents/caregivers in making school and literacy priorities in their homes. Educators must establish a climate of mutual respect and support for all families.

What Is Family Literacy?

Family literacy is a broad, complex construct that generally includes four areas: 1. activities that foster literacy behaviors between parents/caregivers and their children; 2. direct instruction in literacy strategies for parents/caregivers to implement with children; 3. adult literacy instruction; and 4. early intervention programs for preschool children (Wasik and Van Horn 2012). Early Start and Head Start are examples of extensive intervention programs that deliver all four components in order to help children who may be at risk for experiencing difficulty in elementary school. But family literacy extends beyond school-based activities completed in the home. It encompasses the functional use of oral, written, computer, mathematical, and other types of literacy within families. Unfortunately, teacher preparation programs have few, if any, courses dedicated to studying the concepts of family literacy and its impact on student achievement, or ways to develop effective family literacy programs in schools (Graue and Brown 2003). Professional development that encourages educators to learn about—and reflect on—the ethnic, racial, and cultural heritage of families can impact instruction for individual students and increase understanding of the varying family dynamics and literacy practices in contemporary homes. Professional development offers educators valuable opportunities to gain knowledge and strategies for cultivating positive home–school connections since this topic is often lacking in pre-service education programs (Broussard 2000; Epstein and Sanders 2006).

Getting Started

The Power of the Home–School Connection is a series of sessions for educators focusing on several aspects of developing a vibrant family literacy program. This information may be offered as one 3.5-hour staff development opportunity or, ideally, as six half-hour sessions, possibly linked to faculty meetings. When delivered over the course of several sessions, teachers and staff hear the message a number of times, which can be more effective than a single session. The facilitator should be someone with knowledge of and vested interest in family literacy. Administrators, classroom teachers, social workers, literacy specialists, teachers of English language learners (ELLs), speech pathologists, teachers of the arts, and other faculty and staff bring valuable insights and viewpoints to discussions, broadening understanding and ultimately the impact of the sessions. Participants explore and expand their awareness of family literacy, various cultural differences, and related issues that must be addressed to benefit students. Participants discuss brief articles with information that pertains to their schools and brainstorm ways to formulate an effective plan of action that will strengthen the home–school connection.

Session 1: What Is Your Family Literacy Schema?

Time: 30 minutes

Supplies

- Tables and chairs for participants
- Copies of Teacher Reflection (See Resource Packet)
- Pencils or pens
- Table assignments to form groups that include various grade levels, subjects, and support personnel
- Chart paper/whiteboard and markers, or computer and projector

Leading the Session

- 5 minutes: Welcome faculty and staff. Introduce the session by reflecting that educators often wish parents and caregivers would be more involved in their students' academic lives. State that the purpose of this session is to explore ways we can make that happen. Read or paraphrase the "What Is Family Literacy?" paragraph (above). Ask participants to reflect and offer comments. Be nonjudgmental; accept all comments. Model the respect we intend parents/caregivers to receive in our schools.
- 15 minutes: State that by examining our backgrounds, we begin a process in which we evaluate the needs of our school families and find ways to work together to meet those needs. Distribute the Teacher Reflection and direct participants to fill out Part 1. When all have completed the questionnaire, ask participants to discuss Parts 2, 3, and 4 with table mates. Request that each table choose a Reporter.
- 10 minutes: As each group shares the salient points of their discussion of Part 4, record the statements on chart paper/whiteboard, or computer.
- Briefly note the common themes.
- If this is Session 1 of multiple day sessions, thank all for coming. Otherwise, continue to Session 2.

Session 2: What Do We Need to Know about Families' Literacy Practices in the Home? Part 1

Time: 30 minutes

Supplies
- Tables and chairs for participants
- Copies of the Teacher Perspective (See Resource Packet)
- Copies of the articles and books to display; choose one to discuss (See Resource Packet)
- Pencils or pens
- Table assignments to form groups that include various grade levels, subjects, and support personnel

Leading the Session
- 2 minutes: Welcome participants. State that before we can expect parents/caregivers to be open to suggestions to improve home–school communication and build better relationships, we need to appreciate and demonstrate respect for the cultural differences of the families in our school. Teachers may not have extensive knowledge of various cultures represented in the school population (religious, gender, poverty, race, ethnicity), yet cultural differences affect the home life, belief system, and perhaps the parent/caregiver and student's view of school and the value of education (Davis et al. 2005). Embracing cultural differences promotes empathy, develops understanding, and fosters real-life learning opportunities in schools.
- 3 minutes: Distribute Teacher Perspective page. Direct participants to read the statements and indicate their opinion.
- 10 minutes: Distribute one of the suggested articles and allow participants a few minutes to read the article. Another effective approach is to read aloud one of the suggested picture books. (See list in Resource Packet.)
- 15 minutes: Ask participants to reflect on the reading or book. Does the information cause them to rethink the rating of any of the five statements? Encourage sharing of ideas, feelings, and frustrations in a nonjudgmental atmosphere.
- If this is Session 2 of multiple day sessions, thank all for coming. Otherwise, offer a 15-minute break before continuing to Session 3.

Session 3: What Do We Need to Know about Families' Literacy Practices in the Home? Part 2

Time: 30 minutes

Supplies
- Tables and chairs for participants
- Participants should bring their copies of Statement Rating Scale
- Copies of a second article or book; choose one to read and discuss (See Resource Packet)
- Pencils or pens
- Table assignments to form groups that include various grade levels, subjects, and support personnel
- Chart paper/whiteboard and markers, or computer and projector

Leading the Session
- 5 minutes: Welcome participants and review what was discussed in the previous session. Solicit comments and note on chart paper/whiteboard or project via computer.
- 10 minutes: Read aloud the picture book or distribute article for participants to read silently.
- 15 minutes: Ask participants to reflect on the reading and share whether the information contained would change their rating of any of the five statements. Discuss.
  1. What alternative literacy practices may take place in the home?
  2. Why might parents/caregivers seem disengaged in their children's education?
  3. What other valuable learning may be taught in the home?
  4. What effective strategies can teachers use to become informed about and reinforce literacy activities that are taking place in the home?
  5. In what ways may a study of other cultures enhance our classroom?
- 5 minutes: Solicit comments regarding changes in thinking, new understandings, or empathy for parents/caregivers. Note on chart paper/whiteboard or project via computer.
- If this is Session 3 of multiple day sessions, thank all for coming. Otherwise, continue to Session 4.

Session 4: Why and How Do Parents/Caregivers Become Involved in School Culture?

Time: 30 minutes

Supplies
- Tables and chairs for participants
- Pencils or pens
- Copies or projection of the Hoover-Dempsey and Sandler model of the Parental Involvement Process. Link available in eResources online.
- Table assignments to form groups that include various grade levels, subjects, and support personnel
- Chart paper/whiteboard and markers
- Computer and projector (if projecting article)

Leading the Session
- 5 minutes: Welcome participants. State that parents/caregivers may have many reasons for getting involved or not getting involved in their children's schooling. One model to discuss is the Hoover-Dempsey and Sandler Model of the Parental Involvement Process (Hoover-Dempsey and Sandler 1995). Distribute or project handout. (Be sure it is clearly visible.) Ask a participant to note key statements or questions on chart paper/whiteboard.
- 25 minutes: Participants study and discuss the model.
  - Read descriptors of Level 1, 1.5, and 2 to identify our school's strengths and weaknesses in motivating our parents/caregivers to become more involved.
  - Does this model help us better understand the strengths and areas we can improve in our home–school communication and parent/caregiver involvement? How can we meet the specific needs of our parents/caregivers?
- If this is Session 4 of multiple day sessions, thank all for coming. Otherwise, offer a 15-minute break and continue to Session 5.

Session 5: What Are Some Practices We Can Integrate into Our School Culture to Encourage Parents/Caregivers to Become More Involved?

Time: 30 minutes

Supplies
- Tables and chairs for participants
- Pencils or pens
- Copies of Action Descriptions (See Resource Packet.)
- Table assignments to form groups that include various grade levels, subjects, and support personnel
- Chart paper/whiteboard and markers, or computer and projector

Leading the Session
- 5 minutes: Welcome participants. State that in this session they are to read and discuss possible methods for enhancing parent/caregiver communication and involvement.
- 25 minutes: Distribute Action Descriptions. Ask participants to read and discuss in their groups the actions the school already undertakes and other actions that may be possible to implement.
- Add to the list other ideas that arise from discussions.
- If this is Session 5 of multiple day sessions, thank all for coming. Otherwise, continue to Session 6.

Stephen Truitt. Photograph used with permission.

Session 6: What Is Our Plan of Action?

Time: 30 minutes

Supplies
- Tables and chairs for participants
- Pencils or pens
- Participants should bring Action Descriptions handout
- Copies of the Action Plan checklist (See Resource Packet)
- Table assignments to form groups that include various grade levels, subjects, and support personnel
- Chart paper/whiteboard and markers, or computer and projector

Leading the Session
- 5 minutes: Welcome participants. State that the focus of this session is to designate a plan of action to implement ideas that will improve the home–school connection.
- 10 minutes: Distribute Action Plan checklist. Ask participants to review with table mates the Action Descriptions from the previous class and decide if it is already a policy or activity in the school.
- 15 minutes: As a whole group, decide on one or two actions that may be readily implemented. Decide on a time table, person or persons responsible for implementing the action, and methods to measure success. Identify actions that may be put into effect at a future time or become a long-term project. Some activities may not be deemed appropriate or doable. Determine if future meetings are necessary and schedule immediately.
- Thank all for coming and for all their input.
- Follow up with communication on progress of implemented plans.

Bibliography

Broussard, C. Anne, "Preparing Teachers to Work with Families: A National Survey of Teacher Education Programs," *Equity and Excellence in Education* 33, no. 2 (2000): 41–49, doi:10.1080/1066568000330207

Colby, Susan A. and Anna F. Lyon, "Heightening Awareness About the Importance of Using Multicultural Literature," *Multicultural Education* 11, no. 3 (Spring 2004): 24–28.

Davis, Kathryn L., Bernice G. Brown, Ann Liedel-Rice, and Pamela Soeder, "Experiencing Diversity Through Children's Multicultural Literature," *Kappa Delta Pi Record* 41, no. 4 (Summer 2005): 176–179, doi:10.1080/00228958.2005.10532067

Dunsmore, Kailonnie and Douglas Fisher, eds., *Bringing Literacy Home*. Newark, DE: International Reading Association, 2010.

Edwards, Patricia A., "Combining Parents' and Teachers' Thoughts About Storybook Reading at Home and School," in *Family Literacy: Multiple Perspectives to Enhance Literacy Development*, ed. L. M. Morrow, Newark, DE: International Reading Association, 1995.

Epstein, Joyce L. and Susan L. Dauber, "School Programs and Teacher Practices of Parent Involvement in Inner-city Elementary and Middle Schools," *Elementary School Journal* 91 (1991): 289–305, doi:10.1086/461656

Epstein, Joyce L. and Mavis G. Sanders, "Prospects for Change: Preparing Educators for School, Family, and Community Partnerships," *Peabody Journal of Education* 81, no. 2 (2006): 81–120, doi:10.1207/S15327930pje8102_5

Fan, Xitao and Michael Chen, "Parental Involvement and Students' Academic Achievement: A Meta-analysis," *Educational Psychology Review* 13, no. 1 (2001): 1–22, doi:10.1023/A:1009048817385

Graue, M. Elizabeth and Christopher P. Brown, "Preservice Teachers' Views of Families in Education," *Teaching & Teacher Education* 19, no. 7 (October 2003): 719–735, doi:10.1016/j.tate.2003.06.002

Hindin, Alisa and Jeanne R. Paratore, "Supporting Young Children's Literacy Learning Through Home–School Partnerships: The Effectiveness of a Home Repeated-Reading Intervention," *Journal of Literacy Research* 39, no. 3 (October 2007): 307–333, doi:10.1080/10862960701613102

Hoover-Dempsey, Kathleen V. and Howard M. Sandler, "Parental Involvement in Children's Education: Why Does It Make a Difference?" *Teachers College Record* 97, no. 2 (Winter 1995): 310–331.

Lapp, Diane, Douglas Fisher, James Flood, and Kelly Moore, " 'I don't want to teach it wrong': An Investigation of the Role Families Believe They Should Be Playing in the Early Literacy Development of Their Children," *51st Yearbook of the National Reading Conference*, 275–287, Oak Creek, Wisconsin, 2002.

Moll, Luis C. and James B. Greenberg, "Creating Zones of Possibilities: Combining Social Contexts for Instruction," in *Vygotsky and Education: Instructional Implications and Applications of Sociohistorical Psychology*, ed. Luis C. Moll, New York: Cambridge University Press, 1990, doi:10.1017/CBO9781139173674.016

Sénéchal, Monique, Jo-Anne LeFevre, Eleanor Thomas, and Karen E. Daley, "Differential Effects of Home Literacy Experiences on the Development of Oral and Written Language," *Reading Research Quarterly* 33, no. 1 (January/February/March 1998): 96–116, doi:10.1598/RRQ.33.1.5

Sénéchal, Monique and Laura Young, "The Effect of Family Literacy Interventions on Children's Acquisition of Reading from Kindergarten to Grade 3: A Meta-Analytic Review," *Review of Educational Research* 78, no. 4 (2008): 880–907, doi:10.3102/0034654308320319

Wasik, Barbara H. and Barbara Van Horn, "The Role of Family Literacy in Society," in *Handbook of Family Literacy*, 2nd ed., ed. Barbara Hanna Wasik, 3–18, New York: Routledge, 2012.

Teacher Resource Packet for Staff Development Sessions can be found on the following pages.

Susan E. Busch. Photograph used with permission.

Teacher Resource Packet

Session 1   Teacher Reflection

Part 1

1. What are your first memories of reading at home?

2. What are your first memories of school?

3. When you had difficulty with homework or studying, how did you get assistance?

4. What types of learning activities took place in your home?

Part 2 Discuss: Did these early experiences influence your decision to become a teacher?

Part 3 Discuss: Describe what you believe to be your students' learning environment at home.

Part 4 Discuss and Share: How do students' home experiences/learning environments impact the attitudes and learning of the parents and students in our school?

Session 2: Teacher Perspective

Rate your level of agreement with each statement.

	Totally Agree	Somewhat Agree	Somewhat Disagree	Totally Disagree
1. Our students come from literacy-impoverished homes.				
2. Our parents/caregivers value education.				
3. Existing school programs are adequate; home factors are not.				
4. We need to promote more school-like activities for the home.				
5. Cultural differences can increase learning.				

Sessions 2 and 3:   Suggestions for Participant Readings

- Internet search for "An Indian Father's Plea" or click on link available in eResources online.

- Internet search for "Open Letter to a Non-Indian Teacher" or click on link available in eResources.

- Internet search for "Why Some Parents Don't Come to School" or click on link available in eResources.

- Edwards, Patricia A. "Combining Parents' and Teachers' Thoughts About Storybook Reading at Home and School." In *Family Literacy: Multiple Perspectives to Enhance Literacy Development*, ed. L. M. Morrow, 54. Newark, DE: International Reading Association, 1995.

Children's books:

- *Grandpa, Is Everything Black Bad?*, by Sandy Lynne Holman, illustrated by Lela Kometiani. A young boy questions his heritage. Ages 5–10.

- *I Speak English for My Mom*, by Muriel Stanek, illustrated by Judith Friedman. A young girl translates for her mother who does not speak English. Ages 4–8.

- *Fly Away Home*, by Eve Bunting, illustrated by Ronald Himler. A boy and his dad experience being homeless. Ages 4–8.

- *Tight Times*, by Barbara Shook Hazen, illustrated by Trina Schart Hyman. A young boy copes with his dad's job loss. Ages 5–10.

- *Those Shoes*, by Maribeth Boelts, illustrated by Noah Z. Jones. A child longs for the popular shoes everyone else is wearing but his family is unable to afford. Ages 5–8.

- *Uncle Willie and the Soup Kitchen*, by Dyanne DiSalvo-Ryan. A visit to a soup kitchen opens the eyes of the young child. Ages 4–8.

Session 5: Action Descriptions

Please note that there are no pages in the resource packet for Session 4.

1. Monthly school newsletter: paper or online. Describes all school activities and functions that will take place during that month. May include important articles and learning activities. Write simply; avoid use of "teacher-ese" or acronyms; include icons or graphics for parents/caregivers unable to read English or with limited reading skills.

2. Weekly class newsletter: Contains class activities, units of study, and other important information. Include icons or graphics for parents/caregivers unable to read English.

3. Welcome signs: Visible signs to welcome and direct parents/caregivers to rooms within the school building; include room numbers, arrows, and other languages if there is a population of non-native English-speaking parents/caregivers.

4. Open door policy: Parents/caregivers are always welcome at school with proper notification (exceptions could be during testing, staff development, or meetings). This policy should be discussed and presented in written form at Open House.

5. Formal communication policy: Written explanation of how and when parents/caregivers are best able to contact someone at the school and how the school will contact parents.

6. Parent/caregiver surveys: At least once a year, preferably more often, to gauge the interests, needs, and concerns of parents/caregivers.

7. Parent/caregiver volunteers in all classrooms: Parents/caregivers should be welcomed and involved in classrooms. The school parameters need to be clearly stated.

8. Positive calls home weekly: Typically, parents/caregivers get a phone call only when there is a problem. A policy whereby positive phone calls are made on a regular basis will be welcomed by parents/caregivers.

9. Family literacy logs: Have parents/caregivers and students keep a log or a dated checklist of all kinds of literacy engaged in at home: reading, writing, speaking, and listening. You may have to give parents/caregivers and students lots of examples, such as sang a song, read a recipe, or said prayers. A list might be a good starting point.

10. Home–school journal: May be part of homework; child writes or draws events or activities that take place each day to take home and share. Could be source of journal writing ideas in the classroom.

11. Homework guidelines: Stated guidelines for each grade level, as well as procedures for absences and assistance. Keep language simple.

12. Interactive homework: Specific assignments that engage the entire family. Informs parents/caregivers about what is happening in school and is often more interesting for students to complete.

13. Homework hotline: Setting up a telephone or online service for parents/caregivers and students to get assistance for homework assignments.

14. Parent/caregiver-child dialogue journal: Notebook that goes to school and home on a regular basis for parents/caregivers and students to communicate regarding school activities, events, and work.

15. Parent-teacher conference checklist: Helps parents/caregivers to know the major areas to be discussed and/or information needed; includes space for notes or questions. Parents/caregivers feel empowered if they are prepared ahead of time.

16. Approach parent-teacher conferences positively: Be sure to include time for parent(s)/caregiver(s) and teacher to state positive attributes of student, as well as concerns.

17. Classroom mystery readers: Enlist parents, caregivers, or community leaders to read aloud to a class; clues may be given prior to the reader's arrival to see if students can guess who is coming.

18. Classroom mystery visitors: Encourages parents, caregivers, or community leaders to share expertise or pertinent experiences with the classroom.

19. Classroom cookbook: Parents/caregivers share recipes based on a theme or culture.

20. Child/parent interviews: Brief set of questions encourages parents or other family members to share memories, books, information, etc., even if they cannot come to school during the day.

© 2015, *Empowering Families: Practical Ways to Involve Parents in Boosting Literacy, Grades Pre-K–5*, Judy Bradbury and Susan E. Busch, Routledge.

21. Family of the week: Classroom program informs students of the special nature, traditions, and activities of each family; one family is highlighted each week, possibly on a bulletin board or with a classroom visit.

22. Child notes: Students write notes to parent/caregiver to share learning, insights, and feelings, just as parents/caregivers sometimes write notes for students' lunches or backpacks.

23. Notification of unit of study: Notice or newsletter article that informs parents/caregivers of a particular unit of study and requests photos, souvenirs, books, crafts, etc. to be sent in; parameters must be set ahead of time regarding safety, transportation, and labeling of items.

24. Suggestions for fun activities to do at home: Newsletters, notes, or journals include recipes, experiments, or neighborhood events that parents/caregivers can do with students.

25. Learning games sent home: Purchased or homemade learning games are sent home with directions for playing; it helps if students have played the game at school before sending it home.

26. Thematic literacy backpack: Purchase an inexpensive backpack or sturdy plastic zip bags. Choose a theme and place books, games, articles, or other items in the backpack with a blank notebook. Each week the backpack goes home with a different student. Families are asked to do an activity or two and write a short paragraph about their experience.

27. Family pen pals: Since we live in a very mobile society, develop a writing program to encourage writing to distant family members.

28. Bring your job to school day: a take-off on bring your child to work. Encourage family members to come to school and talk about their jobs: what they do, what education they needed, what responsibilities they have, and what they love about their work.

29. Current events: Each week parents/caregivers help students find and discuss interesting current events on TV, the newspaper, online, or in their neighborhood. Students write a short summary and include why they chose that event. Students share their summaries in class.

30. Parent lending library: Easily accessed bookshelf or file where books can be checked out by parents/caregivers for reading at home.

31. Parent resource library: Easily accessed bookshelf or file with parenting books, articles, and community resources can be available for parents/caregivers. A dedicated display case or hallway bulletin board may also be utilized to distribute information.

32. Initial home calls: Prior to the start of school, teachers will call each family in the class and welcome them to a new school year.

33. Initial home visits: Teachers schedule a home visit with each household to share information about the upcoming school year.

34. Student exit ticket: Each day the student fills out a form that may include two things they learned that day, things with which they had difficulty, the best and the worst things about the day, or questions they had. This ends the "Nothing" response when parents/caregivers ask, "What did you do in school today?" Promotes conversation.

35. School website: Accessible all times of the day to keep parents/caregivers informed regarding upcoming events, activities, and issues. Needs to be updated regularly.

36. Teacher email accounts: Policy should be in place and parents informed about what is appropriate information to be shared, how soon teachers should respond, and limitation of student access.

37. Parent/Caregiver education nights: May be a series of sessions or singular events based on the stated needs/interests of parents/caregivers.

38. Family literacy evenings: School-wide learning events or literacy motivational events.

39. Cultural awareness staff development: Further staff development may be needed to help foster understanding and development of the home–school connections, which will ultimately help students increase learning and school success.

Session 6:   Action Plan

Action	Currently in Place	Immediate Action	Near Future Action	Long-term Action	No Action	Action Date	Person Responsible
Monthly school newsletter							
Weekly class newsletter							
Welcome signs							
Open door policy							
Formal communication policy							
Parent surveys							
Parent volunteers in all classrooms							
Positive calls home weekly							
Family literacy logs							
Home–school journal							
Homework guidelines							
Interactive homework							
Homework hotline							
Parent-child dialogue journal							
Parent-teacher conference checklist							
Approach conferences positively							
Classroom mystery readers							
Classroom mystery visitors							
Classroom cookbook							
Child/parent interviews							
Family of the week							

Child notes					
Notification of unit of study					
Suggestions for fun activities					
Learning games sent home					
Thematic literacy backpack					
Family pen pals					
Bring your job to school day					
Current events					
Parent lending library					
Parent resource library					
Initial home calls					
Initial home visits					
Student exit ticket					
School website					
Teacher email accounts					
Parent education nights					
Family literacy evenings					
Cultural awareness staff development					

Part III

Parent/Caregiver Literacy Booster Meeting: Three-Part Series

CHAPTER 4

Why Should I Read to My Child (and How, When, and Where)?

Session 1
Getting Started and Keeping On

Parents and caregivers naturally want their children to succeed in school. Decades of research conducted in urban, suburban, and rural areas across the country has shown that parents/caregivers absolutely *can* positively impact their children's academic achievement *simply by reading aloud to them on a daily basis!*

Reading aloud to a child not only models those reading skills at the foundation of competencies necessary to tackle school subjects, but it also lengthens attention span and expands conceptual knowledge. The Common Core State Standards support reading aloud as an integral part of English Language Arts (ELA). Reading aloud in the home nurtures a love of reading and books and boosts positive parent-child interactions. Fifteen minutes a day is all it takes.

Parents/caregivers need to know that from as early as birth to as late as high school, reading aloud to their children makes a difference. Yet they needn't worry if they haven't yet made a habit of reading aloud: it's never too early or too late to start. Reinforcing this fact and reassuring parents/caregivers with easy-to-implement techniques for developing a daily read-aloud habit in their home will replace apathy with a can-do attitude. Students will benefit at home—and in the school setting.

The series of Literacy Booster Meetings for parents/caregivers on reading aloud reinforces the vital role adults play in developing lifelong reading skills in children. By demonstrating a variety of simple techniques, the leader will ease the anxiety many parents/caregivers feel about how to help build strong reading skills and foster a love of reading in their children. These tips are easy to implement, and the rewards are great. Reading aloud can become a habit that family members embrace.

Participants in the meeting(s) will have an opportunity to sample outstanding books for children and will learn quick and efficient means of locating worthwhile literature appropriate for a range of ages. Simple, surefire ways to make the home reading-rich will be explained and reinforced through practice. Resource Packets containing age- and topic-specific bibliographies of children's books and a list of resources designed especially for parents/caregivers will aid participants in "getting started and keeping on" their daily read-aloud habit.

Note: This set of Literacy Booster Meetings on reading aloud may be held as three sessions in a series as outlined here, or Session 1 may be conducted as a single stand-alone session.

The Resource Packets for the subsequent read-aloud sessions in this series of Literacy Booster Meetings contain material that can be distributed in other manners if Session 1 is the only read-aloud meeting conducted. They can be distributed as a packet to reinforce or augment the information covered in this Literacy Booster Meeting, or select pages from the packet can be used as backpack stuffers in the weeks following the Session 1 Literacy Booster Meeting.

To highlight key points and discussion questions and to structure this series of meetings as a unit, you may wish to use the PowerPoint presentation in the eResources materials online. **PP** in the outline indicates where a slide may be presented.

Session 1: Getting Started and Keeping On

Grade Levels: Pre-K–5

Time: 1.5 hours

Supplies
- Large room with chairs to seat all comfortably and with clear view to the podium
- Chart paper/whiteboard and markers
- Copies of Resource Packet
- Children's books for parents/caregivers to browse; see Recommended Read-Alouds listed in the Resource Packet
- Read-aloud book
- Document reader, opaque projector, or another means for sharing the read-aloud book
- Paper/pencils/pens
- A pocketed folder for each participant to store materials distributed at this meeting and for notes they may wish to take (optional)
- PowerPoint presentation and necessary equipment (optional; see PowerPoint presentation in eResources online)
- Light refreshments (optional)

Goals
- Participants will learn about the importance of reading aloud to their children.
- Participants will review a set of simple tips for how to read aloud effectively.
- Participants will listen to a read-aloud of a children's book and discuss the merits and benefits of reading aloud to children.
- Participants will peruse children's books and discuss their merits for reading aloud.

Planning for Literacy Booster Meeting

Several weeks in advance

❑ Select date and reserve a room with adequate space. Internet access is recommended but not required.

❑ Arrange for equipment: a long table to be placed at the front of room on which to display children's books, chairs, and podium. Also include computer, projector, and screen if conducting PowerPoint presentation.

❑ Review PowerPoint presentation (optional).

❑ Announce to faculty and staff; solicit support, participation, and assistance.

❑ Send home invitation of Literacy Booster Meeting. List pertinent details including date, time, and purpose of meeting.

❑ Arrange for publicity via the school website and calendar, classroom calendars, announcements, and school parent organization communications.

❑ As event draws near, distribute simple registration form to be returned to the school. Prominently list response date to facilitate preparation of the room and ensure ample materials. If childcare or transportation will be provided, give details. (See Resource Packet.)

❑ Arrange for a childcare room; solicit volunteers to staff (optional).

One week in advance

❑ Send reminder to families.

❑ Confirm room.

❑ Arrange for refreshments.

❑ Confirm childcare and transportation arrangements, if applicable.

❑ Make copies of Resource Packet.

❑ Gather and become familiar with children's books.

❑ Practice the read-aloud. See detailed suggestions for discussion at the end of this chapter.

The day of the event

❑ Set up necessary equipment (projector, screen, books, materials to disseminate, pens or pencils).

❑ Display children's books on a large table at the front of the room.

❑ Arrange chairs for participants in a way that allows for easy viewing of screen and also facilitates discussion.

❑ Gather refreshments for break (optional).

❑ Check childcare and transportation arrangements, if provided.

Leading the Literacy Booster Meeting

○ Warmly and enthusiastically greet parents/caregivers as they arrive. Encourage browsing of books on display.

○ 5 minutes: **Begin promptly** with a welcome and a reminder to silence cell phones. Circulate the attendance sheet. Review location of restrooms and fire/emergency exit details.

○ 10 minutes: **Overview of Meeting**

• Introduce staff present at the meeting.

• Encourage participants to ask questions and share comments pertinent to the topic throughout the meeting.

• Review schedule for the meeting.

• State the goals for the meeting. See above. **(PP)**

• Ask parents/caregivers to introduce themselves, state the ages of their children, and tell why they signed up for and what they hope to gain from this Literacy Booster Meeting. **(PP)** Note responses briefly on chart paper/whiteboard.

• Draw attention to children's books on display.

• Recite from "The Reading Mother" by Strickland Gillilan **(PP)**:
   "You may have tangible wealth untold;
   Caskets of jewels and coffers of gold.
   Richer than I you can never be—
   I had a Mother who read to me."

• Distribute Resource Packet and briefly overview contents.

○ 10 minutes: **Memory Activity**

• Introduce this activity by asking participants to close their eyes and visualize a time when they were read aloud to by a parent/caregiver, teacher, or family friend. **(PP)** Or, they may wish to bring to mind an instance of reading aloud to one of their children. Ask participants to recall where they were, what time of year it was, the feelings they experienced, and the book. Maintain silence for a minute or so. Next, ask participants to briefly jot down details of their memory on the page in their Resource Packet.

• After 2–3 minutes, offer a personal read-aloud memory. Ask a few volunteers to share their memories.

• Comment positively; reinforce salient points; encourage brief discussion.

○ 15 minutes: **Read-aloud** option one: *The Gruffalo*, by Julia Donaldson, illustrated by Alex Scheffler—a delightful tale in which a wily mouse outwits one ominous character after another. The mouse's triumphs are sure to please any preschooler or primary student. Mention that offered online are many activities related to the book. We'll be looking at such websites in our next session.

- Option two: If this meeting takes place on a cold and wintry evening, you may wish to opt for *Owl Moon*, by Jane Yolen, illustrated by John Schoenherr. This classic picture book is superbly simple: A parent demonstrates his love through the time he spends making a memory with his child.
  - Ask participants to "go back in time" again, imagining themselves as four or five years old as you read them the story.
  - Whichever book you choose, practice reading it aloud beforehand. Read with expression! Model the read-aloud behaviors you hope to foster in participants. This is crucial.
  - As you read the story, pose questions one might ask of young listeners about the storyline, text, and illustrations. See suggestions at the end of this chapter.
  - After reading the story aloud, ask participants to reflect on the read-aloud experience. (**PP**) Note responses on chart paper/whiteboard. Ask:
    - Did you enjoy the experience?
    - What are some things you noticed I did as I read the story aloud that you might try when you read to your children?
    - What did you find surprising, interesting, or helpful from this exercise?
    - What did you like about the story?
- 10 minutes: **Read-Aloud Tips**
  - Review and discuss the read-aloud tips in the Resource Packet.
  - Encourage feedback and sharing of personal experiences.
- 10 minutes: **Break**
  - Offer refreshments (optional).
  - Encourage participants to browse children's books.
- 5 minutes: **Discussion**
  - Following the break, ask participants to form small groups for discussion. Pose these prompts (**PP**):
    - Thinking about what we have learned so far, share with your group what you think is important to remember when reading aloud to your children.
    - Which techniques I used worked well? What caught your attention? What did you enjoy most? Why?
    - Thinking of your own children, what might they like about a daily read-aloud experience?
  - Circulate the room and visit groups.
  - Return to the whole group.
- 15 minutes: **Application**
  - Ask participants to choose a book from the table.
  - Give participants 5 minutes to read through the book they have chosen and consider if they would read it aloud to their child. Why/why not?

- Reconvene.
- Spend 10 minutes sharing books. Ask willing participants to hold up the book they chose so all can see the cover. Ask them to read the title and briefly tell the group about the book, offering a summary of the story, and what they liked (or didn't like) about the book. Show one or two pages. **(PP)** As parents/caregivers present, add brief insights into the book's key elements. Suggest a range of ages for which the book is appropriate.
  - ○ 10 minutes: **Close the session**
    - Review goals of meeting. **(PP)**
    - Review what parents/caregivers hoped to gain from meeting, as noted on chart paper/whiteboard.
    - Ask: What is one thing you will take away from this meeting?
    - If this is the first in a series of read-aloud Literacy Booster Meetings, offer a brief overview of what will be covered in Session 2 and inform participants of the date. **(PP)**
    - Read aloud *Kiss Good Night*, by Amy Hest, illustrated by Anita Jeram.
    - To kick off their read-aloud habit, suggest parents/caregivers read aloud to their children tonight, listen to a book on CD, or visit a website to listen to a book together. (See suggestion in Resource Packet.)
    - Ask participants to complete a brief evaluation of the meeting in order to offer valuable feedback for future meetings. (See Appendix for an example of an evaluation form.)
    - Thank participants for attending.
    - Conclude meeting on time.

Stephen Truitt. Photograph used with permission.

Read-Aloud: Suggested Questions and Story Features to Highlight

The Gruffalo

In this deliciously humorous story told in rhyme, a sly mouse outfoxes a fox in the opening pages. But that's only the beginning of the fun. The mouse addresses the listener/reader and we are in on the secret. We move through the deep, dark woods with the wily little guy, thoroughly entertained by his escapades as he cunningly overcomes one threat after another right through to the story's satisfying end.

Pre-Reading: Show the cover of the book. Explore the inside covers. Ask: Where does this story take place? Return to the cover. Ask: What do you see? What is happening here? Read the title. Ask: What is a gruffalo? Let's read to find out!

While Reading: Read the first page. Ask: What do you think the fox has in mind? Read the next two pages. Ask: Why did the fox run away? Continue reading the story through the mouse's encounter with the snake. Be sure to use expression when reading the line, "There's no such thing as a gruffal . . ." Turn the page dramatically to reveal the spread. Ask: What do you think the mouse will do now? Read to the end of the story.

Follow Up: Ask: Which is your favorite character? Why? What words would you use to describe the mouse? What did you like about this story? What is the best part? Turn to the back flap. Here the author reveals that she first intended to use a tiger in the story. When she realized how hard it was to rhyme tiger with other words, she created the gruffalo! Find the words in the story that rhyme with gruffalo.

Inform participants that online they can access fun activities related to this story. We'll look at some of those websites and others in our next session.

Owl Moon

This is an excellent book for modeling read-aloud techniques. To channel the setting, turn down the lights before you begin to read. Tell participants to imagine they are in the woods at night in the middle of the winter. There is a full moon above, just like the one on the cover. On the very first page the tone is set. As you read the story aloud, use hushed tones, broken only by the "Whoo-whoo-who-who-who-whoooooo" of Pa's calls. The hooting demonstrates reading with expression at its best!

Pre-Reading: Hold up the book so all can view the cover. Read the title. Ask: What time of day is it? What season is it? How do we know?

While Reading: Sustain the mood of this story by reading the book in its entirety without interruption; don't pause for questions. Besides reading in hushed tones, shiver when the child is cold. Endeavor to convey the wintry outing throughout the read-aloud.

Follow Up: After reading the story, ask: Who has seen a real owl? Has anyone seen a great horned owl? Turn to the page where the owl is shown. How would you feel if you saw this owl in the woods? Why did the characters go owling at night? (Introduce the word *nocturnal*. Note that owls are nocturnal, or active at night.) What other animals are nocturnal? (raccoons, skunks) Select and re-read a few of the comparisons made in the story and ask listeners to think of other ways they might describe that feeling. Put the book down and get listeners up! Be trees "still as statues" and "bumping shadows." Shrug, "make your own heat," and best of all—hoot to the owl!

Gene Bradbury. Photograph used with permission.

Bibliography

Anderson, Richard C., Elfrieda H. Hiebert, Judith A. Scott, Ian. A.G. Wilkinson, et. al., *Becoming a Nation of Readers: The Report of the Commission on Reading*. Washington, D.C.: National Institute of Education, 1985.

Bradbury, Judy, *Children's Book Corner: A Read-Aloud Resource with Tips, Techniques, and Plans for Teachers, Librarians, and Parents, Level Pre-K–K*. Westport, CT: ABC-CLIO, 2003.

Bradbury, Judy, *Children's Book Corner: A Read-Aloud Resource with Tips, Techniques, and Plans for Teachers, Librarians, and Parents, Grades 1 and 2*. Westport, CT: ABC-CLIO, 2004.

Bradbury, Judy, *Children's Book Corner: A Read-Aloud Resource with Tips, Techniques, and Plans for Teachers, Librarians and Parents, Grades 3 and 4*. Westport, CT: ABC-CLIO, 2005.

Bradbury, Judy, *Children's Book Corner: A Read-Aloud Resource with Tips, Techniques, and Plans for Teachers, Librarians, and Parents, Grades 5 and 6*. Westport, CT: ABC-CLIO, 2006.

Bradbury, Judy, *Read-Aloud Scaffold: Best Books to Enhance Content Area Curriculum, Grades Pre-K–3*. Santa Barbara, CA: Libraries Unlimited, 2011.

Binkley, Marilyn, et al., *Becoming a Nation of Readers: What Parents Can Do*. Lexington, MA: D.C. Heath, 1988.

Children's Reading Foundation, "For Families," accessed May 30, 2014, www.readingfoundation. org/parents.jsp

Codell, Esmé Raji, *How to Get Your Child to Love Reading*. Chapel Hill, NC: Algonquin, 2003.

Cullinan, Bernice E., *Read to Me: Raising Kids Who Love to Read*. New York: Scholastic, 1992.

Dunsmore, KaiLonnie and Douglas Fisher, eds., *Bringing Literacy Home*. Newark, DE: International Reading Association, 2010.

Durkin, Dolores, *Teaching Them to Read*. Boston: Allyn and Bacon, 1970.

Duursma, E., Marilyn Augustyn, and Barry S. Zuckerman, "Reading Aloud to Children: The Evidence." *Archives of Disease in Childhood* 93, no. 7 (July 2008): 554–557, accessed May 30, 2014, http://adc.bmj.com/content/93/7.toc

Fox, Mem, *Reading Magic: Why Reading Aloud to Our Children Will Change Their Lives Forever*. San Diego, CA: Harcourt, 2001.

Gross, Jacquelyn, *Make Your Child A Lifelong Reader: A Parent-Guided Program for Children of All Ages Who Can't, Won't, or Haven't Yet Started to Read*. New York: St. Martin's Press, 1986.

Hahn, Mary Lee, *Reconsidering Read-Aloud*. Portland, ME: Stenhouse, 2002.

Hart, Betty and Todd R. Risley, *Meaningful Differences in the Everyday Experience of Young American Children*. Baltimore, MD: Paul H. Brookes, 1995.

Jones, Claudia, *Parents Are Teachers, Too: Enriching Your Child's First Six Years*. Charlotte, VT: Williamson, 1988.

Krashen, Stephen D., *The Power of Reading: Insights from the Research*, 2nd ed. Portsmouth, NH: Heinemann/Libraries Unlimited, 2004.

Nash, Jennie, *Raising a Reader: A Mother's Tale of Desperation and Delight*. Santa Barbara, CA: St Martin's Press, 2003.

Quindlen, Anna, *How Reading Changed My Life*. New York: Ballantine, 1998.

Serafini, Frank and Cyndi Giorgis, *Reading Aloud and Beyond: Fostering the Intellectual Life with Older Readers*. Portsmouth, NH: Heinemann, 2003.

Sizer, Michael, "The Surprising Meaning and Benefits of Nursery Rhymes," Public Broadcasting Service, accessed May 30, 2014, www.pbs.org/parents/education/reading-language/reading-tips/the-surprising-meaning-and-benefits-of-nursery-rhymes/

Strickland, Dorothy S. and Lesley Mandel Morrow, eds., *Emerging Literacy: Young Children Learn to Read and Write*. Newark, DE: International Reading Association, 1989.

Trelease, Jim, *Hey! Listen to This: Stories to Read Aloud*. New York: Penguin, 1992.

Trelease, Jim, *The New Read-Aloud Handbook*. New York: Penguin, 1989.

Wasik, Barbara Hanna, ed., *Handbook of Family Literacy*, 2nd ed. New York: Routledge, 2012.

Resource Packet for Why Should I Read to My Child? Session 1: Getting Started and Keeping On can be found on the following pages. See also related Take-Home TipSheets in Chapter 12. TipSheets in color and in Spanish can be found in eResources online.

Join us as we explore surefire ways to help our children become star students and lifelong readers!

Why Should I Read to My Child? (and How, When, and Where)

Getting Started and Keeping On

_____

Date and time

_____

Place

Please return registration form by

_____

Date

Yes, I/we will attend **Why Should I Read to My Child?**

Parent(s)/Caregiver(s) _____

Teacher _____ Room _____

Number of adults attending _____

Number of children for childcare _____

Session 1
Parent/Caregiver
Resource Packet

Parents and Caregivers:
Powerful Partners
in the
Home–School Connection

When you're talking about books, you're never just talking about books. You're talking about life.

—Anna Quindlen, *How Reading Changed My Life*

Did you know . . .

- ➤ Children with an understanding of print, language, and information about the world hit the ground running when they begin school.

  A *Good Goal*: **1,006**: See that your child hears at least **1,000 stories** and knows at least **six nursery rhymes** before the kindergarten bus rolls up to your corner.

- ➤ Older kids who don't read are uninformed about their world—not only current events, but also science and culture—the kind of knowledge that makes for well-rounded, involved citizens who lead productive lives.

  A *Good Goal*: **Hands on!** Purchase magazines of interest to your preteen and teen, or check them out of the library. Be on the lookout for books on topics your child is interested in. Check thrift stores and garage sales and bring home a bundle.

- ➤ The more you read, the better you read. Research shows that **good reading habits = strong reading skills = success in school and the workplace.** Win-win-win. People who read more do better—from earning higher incomes, to staying out of trouble with the law, to doing more charitable work, to getting more exercise!

- ➤ Reading aloud to your child enhances **listening skills,** builds **vocabulary,** lengthens **attention span,** offers a **wide variety of experiences, prepares children to learn to read, models good reading behaviors,** and is packed with **fun and enjoyment!** *What a powerful package a book is!*

  A GREAT Goal: **Make a difference!** Read aloud to your child every day.

The man who does not read good books has no advantage over the man who cannot read them.

—Mark Twain

Read-Aloud Tips

Parents/caregivers often hear this advice from educators:
Read aloud to your child every day.

Why? Because it's been proven to boost success in school!

Okay, you say, I can do that. But, like anything else, there are a few tricks to reading aloud effectively. No worries, though. They're simple and easy tips to follow.

1. **Read aloud books that appeal to you. Every day.** With your child's interests and attention span in mind, choose a book sure to please. But also choose books that make *you* giggle or sit on the edge of *your* seat, and don't overlook factual books. If you find you want to keep reading even when the pasta is boiling over, it's a winner! If you love the book, your child will pick up on that. If, on the other hand, you are not very interested, you'll probably give that away, too. It's okay to re-read favorites, but try new books, too. Talk with your child about the books you read.

2. **Skim the book or chapter before reading it aloud.** Become familiar with the book so you can read with expression. Draw your child into the story and make it memorable. Laugh! Whisper. Shout! Enjoy the illustrations. Your child will beg you to keep reading and reach for a book the next day. *Good, good, good.* Because we want to **read aloud every day.**

3. **Find a comfy spot free of distractions to enjoy your read-aloud time.** Your daily read-aloud will be 15 minutes your child will look forward to and remember. You're making memories!

4. **Read aloud every day.** And not just with your preschooler, but with your middle schooler, too. **Reading aloud is the single most important thing you can do to improve your child's attitude toward reading.** It's one of the best gifts you can give to your child—and it's free, easy, and valuable. It expands your child's horizons and introduces one of life's most satisfying pleasures: the abundant wonders found between the covers of a book.

So pick up a book and begin to make reading aloud a habit. You'll soon find yourself looking forward to reading daily with your child. *What's going to happen next?* you'll wonder. A love of reading instilled in your child, that's what. Oh yeah, and school success!

Prescription for Read-Aloud Success

❑ Start reading as soon as you bring baby home! Don't stop when your child learns to read, or when your child enters middle school or even high school. Keep a' going! Make reading aloud a loving family tradition.

❑ Keep it fun. Don't read books you feel you should read. Read books you both want to read.

❑ Avoid making reading together an obligation—and never reduce it to a punishment. Both you and your child want to eagerly look forward to this daily activity together.

❑ Talk about the book before, during, and after the read-aloud.

❑ Listen to books on tape or online. One website to consider is http://harpercollinschildrens.com/Kids/GamesAndContests/ListeningRoom.aspx.

❑ Pick a mix of books to keep it interesting. Don't forget fairy tales and humor for the young ones, but reach beyond Disney, Dr. Seuss, and other books your children may know well. Facts are fun, too!

Bedtime Read-Alouds for Preschoolers

- ❖ *10 Minutes Till Bedtime*, by Peggy Rathmann.
- ❖ *At Night*, by Jonathan Bean.
- ❖ *Bedtime for Frances*, by Russell Hoban, illustrated by Garth Williams.
- ❖ *Bedtime for Mommy*, by Amy Krouse Rosenthal, illustrated by LeUyen Pham.
- ❖ *Goodnight Goon*, by Michael Rex.
- ❖ *Good Night, Gorilla*, by Peggy Rathmann.
- ❖ *Good-Night, Me*, by Andrew Daddo, illustrations by Emma Quay.
- ❖ *Goodnight Moon*, by Margaret Wise Brown, illustrated by Clement Hurd.
- ❖ *Good-Night, Owl!*, by Pat Hutchins.
- ❖ *Grandfather Twilight*, by Barbara Berger.
- ❖ *The House in the Night*, by Susan Marie Swanson, illustrated by Beth Krommes.
- ❖ *How Do Dinosaurs Say Good Night?*, by Jane Yolen, illustrated by Mark Teague.
- ❖ *If You Were My Bunny*, by Kate McMullan, illustrated by David McPhail.
- ❖ *It Is Night*, by Phyllis Rowand, illustrated by Laura Dronzek.
- ❖ *Kiss Good Night*, by Amy Hest, illustrated by Anita Jeram.
- ❖ *Night Is Coming*, by W. Nikola-Lisa, illustrated by Jamichael Henterly.
- ❖ *No Jumping on the Bed!*, by Tedd Arnold.
- ❖ *One More Hug for Madison*, by Caroline Jayne Church.
- ❖ *Roar of a Snore*, by Marsha Diane Arnold, illustrated by Pierre Pratt.
- ❖ *Safe, Warm, and Snug*, by Stephen R. Swinburne, illustrated by Jose Aruego and Ariane Dewey.
- ❖ *Sleep, Baby, Sleep*, by Maryann Cusimano Love, illustrated by Maria van Lieshout.
- ❖ *Sleep Tight, Anna Banana!*, by Dominique Roques, illustrated by Alexis Dormal.
- ❖ *Ten, Nine, Eight*, by Molly Bang.
- ❖ *Time for Bed*, by Mem Fox, illustrated by Jane Dyer.
- ❖ *Where Does the Brown Bear Go?*, by Nicki Weiss.

. . . and here are two titles perfect for naptime!

- ❖ *Little Brown Bear Won't Take a Nap!*, by Jane Dyer.
- ❖ *The Napping House*, by Audrey Wood, illustrated by Don Wood.

Have only a minute? Or want to read a minute more? Choose a poem or two!

- ❖ *Go to Bed! A Book of Bedtime Poems*, selected by Lee Bennett Hopkins, illustrated by Rosekrans Hoffman.

"Love You!"
Read-Aloud Hugs for Ages 2–6

❖ *Daddies*, by Dian Curtis Regan, illustrated by Mary Morgan.

❖ *Grammy Lamby and the Secret Handshake*, by Kate Klise, illustrated by M. Sarah Klise.

❖ *Guess How Much I Love You?*, by Sam McBratney, illustrated by Anita Jeram.

❖ *How Do Dinosaurs Say I Love You?*, by Jane Yolen, illustrated by Mark Teague.

❖ *Hugging Hour!*, by Aileen Leijten.

❖ *I Love My Daddy Because . . .*, by Laurel Porter-Gaylord, illustrated by Ashley Wolff.

❖ *I Love You, Little One*, by Nancy Tafuri.

❖ *I Love You, Mouse*, by John Graham, illustrated by Tomie de Paola.

❖ *I Want to Say I Love You*, by Caralyn Buehner, illustrated by Jacqueline Rogers.

❖ *Kitchen Dance*, by Maurie J. Manning.

❖ *Love You Forever*, by Robert Munsch, illustrated by Sheila McGraw.

❖ *Mama, Do You Love Me?*, by Barbara M. Joosse, illustrated by Barbara Lavallee.

❖ *Mama Says: A Book of Love for Mothers and Sons*, by Rob D. Walker, illustrated by Leo and Diane Dillon.

❖ *Oh My Baby, Little One*, by Kathi Appelt, illustrated by Jane Dyer.

❖ *Old Bear and His Cub*, by Olivier Dunrea.

❖ *Saturday Is Dadurday*, by Robin Pulver, illustrated by R. W. Alley.

❖ *So Much!*, by Trish Cooke, illustrated by Helen Oxenbury.

❖ *Taking Care of Mama*, by Mitra Modarressi.

❖ *What Do You Love?*, by Jonathan London, illustrated by Karen Lee Schmidt.

❖ *When Mama Comes Home Tonight*, by Eileen Spinelli, illustrated by Jane Dyer.

❖ *Whistling*, by Elizabeth Partridge, illustrated by Anna Grossnickle Hines.

Getting Ready for Kindergarten
Books to Read Aloud to Preschool Grads

- ❖ *Adventure Annie Goes to Kindergarten*, by Toni Buzzeo, illustrated by Amy Wummer.
- ❖ *Countdown to Kindergarten*, by Alison McGhee, illustrated by Harry Bliss.
- ❖ *First Day, Hooray!*, by Nancy Poydar.
- ❖ *First Day Jitters*, by Julie Danneberg, illustrated by Judy Love.
- ❖ *Kindergarten ABC*, by Jacqueline Rogers.
- ❖ *The Kissing Hand*, by Audrey Penn, illustrated by Ruth E. Harper and Nancy M. Leak.
- ❖ *Little Lola*, by Julie Saab, illustrated by David Gothard.
- ❖ *Llama Llama Time to Share*, by Anna Dewdney.
- ❖ The Miss Bindergarten series, by Joseph Slate, illustrated by Ashley Wolff.
- ❖ *My Kindergarten*, by Rosemary Wells.
- ❖ *The Night Before Kindergarten*, by Natasha Wing, illustrated by Julie Durrell.
- ❖ *The Pirate of Kindergarten*, by George Ella Lyon, illustrated by Lynne Avril.
- ❖ *School Bus*, by Donald Crews.
- ❖ *Sweet Briar Goes to School*, by Karma Wilson, illustrated by LeUyen Pham.
- ❖ *The Ticky-Tacky Doll*, by Cynthia Rylant, illustrated by Harvey Stevenson.

Not-to-Be-Missed List
Great Read-Alouds for Ages 3–7!

❖ *All Pigs Are Beautiful*, by Dick King-Smith, illustrated by Anita Jeram.

❖ *Antarctica*, by Helen Cowcher.

❖ *The Crocodile Blues*, by Coleman Polhemus.

❖ *Duck & Goose* books by Tad Hills.

❖ *Dolphin Talk*, by Wendy Pfeffer, illustrated by Helen K. Davie.

❖ *The Emperor's Egg*, by Martin Jenkins, illustrated by Jane Chapman.

❖ *General Store*, by Rachel Field, illustrated by Giles Laroche.

❖ *Germs Make Me Sick*, by Melvin Berger, illustrated by Marylin Hafner.

❖ *The Great Doughnut Parade*, by Rebecca Bond.

❖ *Hands Can*, by Cheryl Willis Hudson, photos by John-Francis Bourke.

❖ *Have You Seen Trees?*, by Joanne Oppenheim, illustrated by Jean and Mou-Sien Tseng.
Also: *Have You Seen Birds?*

❖ **Hello Reader Science** series, Level 1, several titles by Jean Marzollo.

❖ *A House Is a House for Me*, by Mary Ann Hoberman, illustrated by Betty Fraser.

❖ How Do Dinosaurs . . . , series by Jane Yolen, illustrated by Mark Teague.

❖ *How Rocket Learned to Read*, by Tad Hills.

❖ *I Don't Like to Read!*, by Nancy Carlson.

❖ *In the Tall, Tall Grass*, by Denise Fleming. Also: *In the Small, Small Pond*

❖ *Let's Find It!*, by Katya Arnold.

❖ *Little Mouse's Big Book of Fears*, by Emily Gravett.

❖ *Lyle Walks the Dogs: A Counting Book*, by Bernard Waber, illustrated by Paulis Waber.

❖ *Moon Glowing*, by Elizabeth Partridge, illustrated by Joan Paley.

❖ *My Favorite Time of Year*, by Susan Pearson, illustrated by John Wallner.

❖ *My Friend the Monster*, by Eleanor Taylor.

❖ *One Blue Fish: A Colorful Counting Book*, by Charles Reasoner.

❖ *One Little Kitten*, by Tana Hoban.

❖ *Surprising Sharks*, by Nicola Davies, illustrated by James Croft.

Notes

Children are made readers on the laps of their parents.

—Emilie Buchwald

Why Should I Read to My Child (and How, When, and Where)?

Session 2
Reading Aloud to Older Children and Websites of Interest to Parents, Caregivers, and Kids

Note: **PP** *appears in the outline to indicate where a slide may be presented. PowerPoint presentation can be found in eResources online.*

Grade Levels: 3–5

Time: 1.5 hours

Supplies

- Large room with chairs to seat all comfortably and with clear view to the podium
- Chart paper/whiteboard and markers
- Copies of Resource Packet
- Children's books for parents/caregivers to browse (See Recommended Read-Alouds in the Resource Packet.)
- Read-aloud book
- Document reader, opaque projector, or another means for sharing the read-aloud book
- Paper/pencils/pens
- A pocketed folder for each participant to store materials distributed at this meeting and for notes they may wish to take (optional)
- PowerPoint presentation (optional; see eResources online.)
- Light refreshments (optional)

Goals

- Participants will discuss their experiences reading aloud to their children.
- Participants will review tips for reading aloud effectively.

- Participants will listen to a chapter of a children's book intended for an older child.
- Participants will engage in discussion of tips for reading aloud to older children.
- Participants will review websites focusing on literacy of interest to parents/caregivers.
- Participants will become familiar with opportunities for children to read in and around the home.

Planning for Literacy Booster Meeting

Several weeks in advance

☐ Select date and reserve a room with adequate space. Internet access is recommended but not required.

☐ Arrange for equipment: a long table to be placed at the front of room on which to display children's books; chairs; podium; computer, projector, and screen.

☐ Review PowerPoint presentation (optional).

☐ Announce to faculty and staff; solicit support, participation, and assistance.

☐ Send home inviting announcement of Literacy Booster Meeting Session 2 listing all pertinent details including date, time, and purpose of meeting. Arrange for publicity via the school website and calendar, classroom calendars, announcements, and school parent organization communications.

☐ As event draws near, distribute simple registration form to be returned to the school. Prominently list response date to facilitate preparation of the room and ensure ample materials. If childcare or transportation will be provided, give details. (See sample in Resource Packet.)

☐ Arrange for a childcare room; solicit volunteers to staff. Arrange transportation, if provided (optional).

One week in advance

☐ Send reminder to families.

☐ Confirm room.

☐ Confirm childcare and transportation arrangements, if applicable.

☐ Arrange for refreshments.

☐ Make copies of Resource Packet. Note: It may be helpful to copy the "Read-AloudTips" page from the Session 1 Resource Packet and have it available for participants who did not attend the first session, or add it to the Session 2 packet.

☐ Gather and become familiar with children's books.

☐ Practice read-aloud. See detailed suggestions for discussion of Chapter 1 of *One Crazy Summer* at the end of this chapter.

☐ Become familiar with featured websites.

The day of the event

- ❏ Set up room (projector, screen, books, materials to disseminate, pens or pencils).
- ❏ Display children's books on a large table at the front of the room.
- ❏ Arrange chairs for easy viewing of the screen and to facilitate discussion.
- ❏ Gather refreshments for break (optional).
- ❏ Check on childcare and transportation arrangements, if provided.

Leading the Literacy Booster Meeting

- ○ Warmly and enthusiastically greet parents/caregivers as they arrive. Encourage browsing of books on display.
- ○ 5 minutes: **Begin promptly** with a welcome and a reminder to silence cell phones. Circulate attendance sheet. Review location of restrooms and fire/emergency exit details.
- ○ 10 minutes: **Overview of Meeting**
  - Introduce staff present at the meeting.
  - Ask if there are any questions related to what was covered in the first session. Encourage participants to ask questions and share comments pertinent to the topic throughout the meeting.
  - Review schedule for the meeting.
  - Review the goals for the meeting (see above). **(PP)**
  - Ask parents/caregivers to introduce themselves, state the ages of their children, and tell why they signed up for/what they hope to gain from this second Literacy Booster Meeting focusing on reading aloud. **(PP)** Note briefly on chart paper/whiteboard.
  - Draw attention to children's books on display.
  - Distribute Resource Packet and briefly overview contents.
- ○ 10 minutes: **Recap Read-Aloud Experiences**
  - Ask participants to tell about their read-aloud experiences since the first Read-Aloud Literacy Booster Meeting. Solicit details, such as ages of children, how often they read aloud, how long read-alouds took, and the types or titles of books read aloud.
  - Comment positively; reinforce salient points; encourage brief discussion of what participants found of value in the experiences. Be enthusiastic; reinforce positive comments.
  - Review read-aloud tips and discuss participants' experiences.
  - Note that the last session concentrated primarily on reading to young children. Ask: Do you see yourself reading aloud to your older children?
- ○ 15 minutes: **Read aloud** first chapter of *One Crazy Summer*, by Rita Williams-Garcia.
  - Read with expression! Model the read-aloud behaviors you hope to foster in participants.
  - As you read, pose questions one might ask middle graders about the storyline, setting, action, and characters. See suggestions at the end of this chapter.

- Ask participants to reflect on the read-aloud experience. (**PP**)
  - Did you enjoy the read-aloud of a chapter in a longer book?
  - What do you like about the idea of reading aloud to older children? Why is it valuable?
  - How did this read-aloud differ from a read-aloud for a younger child?
  - What age child would you read this story to? (9–11 years) Note that kids like to read stories about characters who are slightly older than they are. Delphine is 11 years old. When choosing books for middle graders, it's important to review the book to be sure it is appropriate. Consider interest and maturity levels.
  - Discuss the plot, characters, setting, and action. What has the author managed to do in this first chapter?
  - Do you want to keep reading to find out what happens next? Do you think your child would feel this way?
  - What did you find surprising, interesting, or helpful from this exercise?
  - What did you notice I did as I read aloud this chapter that you might try when you read aloud to your older children?
  - Do you see yourself reading aloud to your older children?
  - Note Recommended Read-Alouds for older children in the Resource Packet.
  - Encourage participants to try reading aloud to their older children. Caution that it might take some time getting older children used to the routine. Don't give up!
- 10 minutes: **Reading Aloud to Older Children**. Refer to page in handout. Encourage participants to engage in discussion of bullet points.
- 10 minutes: **Break**
  - Offer refreshments (optional).
  - Encourage participants to browse children's books on display.
- 20 minutes: **Literacy Boosting Websites**
  - Ask participants to turn to the page in the Resource Packet that lists websites focusing on literacy. Suggest they take notes on the sites of particular interest as you explore them.
  - Introduce each site. If Internet access is available, open the link. Offer an overview of the site and its function and value. Navigate through the site, highlighting points of interest. Solicit comments; encourage discussion.
- 10 minutes: **Close the session**
  - Review goals of meeting. (**PP**)
  - Ask: What is one thing you will take away from this meeting?
  - Briefly overview what will be covered in the final session in this series of Literacy Booster Meetings and inform participants of the date. (**PP**)
  - Encourage parents/caregivers to read to their older children tonight.
  - Ask participants to complete a brief evaluation of the meeting in order to offer valuable feedback for future meetings. (See Appendix for an example of an evaluation form.)
  - Thank participants for attending.
  - Conclude meeting on time.

Read-Aloud: Suggested Questions and Story Features to Highlight

One Crazy Summer

Chapter 1: "Cassius Clay Clouds"

This novel has garnered a slew of awards, including a Newbery Honor, the Coretta Scott King Award, and National Book Award Finalist. The story is set in the summer of 1968. Main character Delphine is 11 years old and the eldest of three sisters living with their grandmother and father in Brooklyn. As the story opens, the sisters are on their way to spend the summer with their mother, Cecile, who abandoned the family when Delphine was four years old and her littlest sister Fern was an infant. The events that occur in the summer of 1968 in Oakland, CA, and the memorable characters will stay with you beyond the last page of this novel. There's a sequel, too (*P.S. Be Eleven*), so middle graders who fall in love with the characters can read further adventures!

Pre-Reading: Ask participants to imagine themselves to be a middle grader. Show the cover and read the title. Ask: What do you see on the cover? (Lots of stickers for awards, three characters, urban setting.) Explain: This story takes place in 1968. Afros, Black Panthers, and a summer camp sponsored by revolutionaries are woven into the tale of three sisters and how they reconcile with the mother who abandoned them. Let's meet the sisters!

While Reading: Read the first chapter. Use pauses to accentuate humor and emotional moments. Channel Delphine in your tone! Vary voice for Delphine's memories.

Follow Up:
- Ask: What have we learned in this first chapter? (who the main characters are, where they live, where they are going, the circumstances of this trip, the time period in which the story is set, a bit of American history)
- Review the characters we meet or hear about in the first chapter (narrator, Delphine Vonetta; Fern; Big Mama; Pa; Cecile; Uncle Darnell).
- Ask: Who is telling the story? What do we know from Delphine's narration? (Cecile abandoned family; kids are afraid to fly; Big Mama is sad to see the girls get on the plane; Big Mama is religious; Uncle Darnell likes Cecile, though the rest of the adults do not; Cecile is not a loving mom; sisters are heading to California to stay with Cecile for the summer).
- Explain: This story is historical fiction. It takes place at a time in U.S. history, and while historical figures mentioned in the story are real (such as Cassius Clay or Muhammad Ali, and President and Jackie Kennedy), the characters in the story are fictional, or imaginary. Ask: What history does the reader learn from this chapter?
- What do you think readers find out in Chapter 2? Do you want to keep reading? Why?

Resource Packet for Why Should I Read to My Child? Session 2: Reading Aloud to Older Children and Websites of Interest to Parents, Caregivers, and Kids can be found on the following pages. See also related Take-Home TipSheets in Chapter 12. TipSheets in color and in Spanish can be found in eResources online.

Susan E. Busch. Photograph used with permission.

Join us as we continue to explore surefire ways to help our children become star students and lifelong readers!

Why Should I Read to My Child?
Session 2

Reading Aloud to Older Kids and Websites of Interest to Parents, Caregivers, and Kids

_____
Date and time

_____
Place

Please return registration form by

_____
Date

- -

Yes, I/we will attend **Why Should I Read to My Child? Session 2**

Parent(s)/Caregiver(s) _____

Teacher _____ Room _____

Number of adults attending _____

Number of children for childcare _____

Session 2
Parent/Caregiver
Resource Packet

Not-to-Be-Missed List
Great Read-Aloud Choices for Ages 8–11!

❖ *Because of Winn-Dixie*, by Kate DiCamillo.
❖ *Breathing Room*, by Marsha Hayles.
❖ *Diary of a Wimpy Kid* series, by Jeff Kinney.
❖ *Fever 1793*, by Laurie Halse Anderson.
❖ *Frindle*, by Andrew Clements.
❖ *Frogged*, by Vivian Vande Velde.
❖ *The Hero of Third Grade*, by Alice DeLaCroix.
❖ *Joey Pigza* books, by Jack Gantos.
❖ *Locomotion*, by Jacqueline Woodson.
❖ *A Long Walk to Water*, by Linda Sue Park.
❖ *Love That Dog*, by Sharon Creech.
❖ *Masters of Disaster*, by Gary Paulsen.
❖ *One Crazy Summer*, by Rita Williams-Garcia. See also sequel: *P.S. Be Eleven.*
❖ *The Phantom Tollbooth*, by Norman Juster.
❖ *Pigs Might Fly*, by Dick King-Smith, illustrated by Mary Rayner.
❖ *Sahara Special*, by Esmé Raji Codell.
❖ *Sideways Stories from Wayside School*, by Louis Sachar.
❖ *The Storm in the Barn*, by Matt Phelan.
❖ *The Time Warp Trio* series, by Jon Scieszka, illustrated by Lane Smith.
❖ *The Underneath*, by Kathi Appelt.
❖ *The Watsons Go to Birmingham—1963*, by Christopher Paul Curtis.
❖ *When You Reach Me*, by Rebecca Stead.

Tips for Reading Aloud to Middle Graders 8–11 Years Old

○ Be patient as you develop the routine if you haven't made a habit of reading aloud to your middle grader.

○ Do not read too much or for too long at first—gradually lengthen reading time to increase attention span.

○ Choose a distraction-free location.

○ Keep it fun!

○ Don't ask your child to read to you; it's your turn during this special together time.

○ If a book doesn't seem to be holding your child's interest after a few chapters, move on to another book. Laboring through a book defeats the purpose!

○ Encourage your older child to choose the book you'll read aloud.

○ End the read-aloud session at a suspenseful point in the book. Usually, this occurs at the end of a chapter.

○ Vary the types of books you read. Choose a mystery, and then go for a factual book or a fantasy next!

○ Share interesting magazines or news articles during read-aloud time.

○ Following a book you've read aloud, encourage your child to read another book by the author independently—and then choose a different book for your next read-aloud.

○ If your older child balks at being read to, consider independently reading the same book—either one assigned in school or one your child chooses. Discuss pivotal passages or share sections with appealing language or sensory images.

Literacy Is Power!

Resources for Parents/Caregivers

Did you know . . . Experts believe that a child who can recite a few nursery rhymes by the time he or she is four years old most likely will be among the best readers in 3rd grade.

To learn more about the benefits of reading to your little one, check out these books written for parents/caregivers:

- ✓ *Babies Need Books*, revised edition, by Dorothy Butler.
- ✓ *Hey! Listen to This: Stories to Read-Aloud*, by Jim Trelease.
- ✓ *How to Get Your Child to Love Reading*, by Esmé Raji Codell.
- ✓ *Let's Read About . . . Finding Books They'll Love to Read*, by Bernice Cullinan.
- ✓ *Michele Landsberg's Guide to Children's Books*, by Michele Landsberg.
- ✓ *The Read-Aloud Handbook*, 7th edition, by Jim Trelease.
- ✓ *Parents Are Teachers, Too*, by Claudia Jones.
- ✓ *A Parent's Guide to Children's Reading*, by Nancy Larrick.
- ✓ *Read to Me: Raising Kids Who Love to Read*, by Bernice Cullinan.
- ✓ *Reading Magic: Why Reading Aloud to Our Children Will Change Their Lives Forever*, by Mem Fox.

Websites:

- ❖ **www.readingrainbow.com/** *Reading Rainbow* website includes information on a free app for "an unlimited library of books and video field trips."
- ❖ **http://pbskids.org/** PBS has put together a great interactive site for kids, including videos, games, and a link to sign up for their free newsletter, *PBS KIDS Insider*, chock-full of "tips, crafts, recipes, and more."
- ❖ **www.trelease-on-reading.com/** This is the website of reading advocate and best-selling author of *The Read-Aloud Handbook*, Jim Trelease, where "the goal is to help children make books into friends, not enemies." Site features reviews of children's books, a message to dads, perspectives on censorship, a video for reluctant preteen and teen readers on "how to read a book you DON'T want to read," and more.
- ❖ **www.nea.org/home/ParentPartnershipResources.html** Website of the National Education Association offers a variety of resources for parents/caregivers, many of them downloadable and some offered in Spanish.
- ❖ **www.parenting.com/blogs/mom-congress/melissa-taylor/10-best-educational-websites-kids-are-free** *Parenting* lists its choice of 10 best free educational websites.

❖ http://ecs.ovec.org/documents/Reading_Websites_For_Parents.pdf Download "Reading Websites for Parents" here.

❖ www.readingrockets.org/audience/parents This popular educational site has a page for parents/caregivers.

❖ http://gws.ala.org/ The American Library Association spotlights a Best Site of the Week on its Great Websites for Kids page and also categorizes recommended sites according to subjects and interest areas tabbed along the top of the page.

❖ www.wegivebooks.com/ Find a wide variety of books to share with your children on this website.

Google your children's **favorite authors and illustrators** to locate their official websites. Many offer age-appropriate activities related to their books, funny or interesting anecdotes about their lives or the making of their books, and other information related to what they've written and/or illustrated. Here are a few examples:

❖ We read *The Gruffalo* together at Session 1. Visit **www.gruffalo.com/**, the official site for *The Gruffalo*, to meet the author, find games and competitions, and more. You can hear the author of *The Gruffalo*, Julia Donaldson, and her husband perform "The Gruffalo's Child Song" at **www.gruffalo.com/join-in/songs/**. You can also print the lyrics to the song. Go to **www.gruffalo.com/join-in/activities/** for instructions on how to make a gruffalo mask, finger puppets, and even a gruffalo cake. Find plenty of additional fun activities collected here: **http://rubberbootsandelfshoes.blogspot.com/2012/11/have-you-seen-gruffalo.html**.

❖ Mo Willems is the beloved author of many books for preschoolers and primary grade students, including *Don't Let the Pigeon Drive the Bus, Knuffle Bunny* (K is pronounced!), and the Elephant and Piggie series. Visit Willem's interactive site: **www.mowillems.com/** and Pigeon's personal website: **www.pigeonpresents.com/**.

❖ Developed by popular children's writer Jon Scieszka, **www.guysread.com** is especially for boys! Its mission is "to help boys become self-motivated, lifelong readers."

Always monitor your children's use of the Internet.
To purchase books online: **www.amazon.com;**
www.barnesandnoble.com

And last but not least . . .
Librarians and **teachers** are reliable resources, eager to partner with you to serve your child's reading needs.

Notes

The reading habit is a personal thing; a home and family thing.

—Marion Lloyd

Why Should I Read to My Child (and How, When, and Where)?

Session 3
Reading Together Here, There, and Every-Which-Where!

*Note: **PP** appears in the outline to indicate where a slide may be presented. PowerPoint presentation can be found in eResources online.*

Grade Levels: Pre-K–5

Time: 1.5 hours

Supplies
- Large room with chairs to seat all comfortably and with clear view to the podium
- Chart paper/whiteboard and markers
- Copies of Resource Packet
- Children's poetry books for parents/caregivers to browse (See Recommended Read-Alouds in the Resource Packet.)
- Read-aloud book
- Document reader, opaque projector, or another means for sharing the read-aloud book
- Paper/pencils/pens
- A pocketed folder for each participant to store materials distributed at this meeting and for notes they may wish to take (optional)
- PowerPoint presentation (optional; see eResources online.)
- Light refreshments (optional)
- Wrapped candies or festive pencils for poetry writing activity (optional)

Goals
- Participants will review tips for reading aloud effectively.
- Participants will become familiar with opportunities for children to read in and around the home.

- Participants will engage in discussion of everyday opportunities to read with children.
- Participants will discuss their experiences reading poetry.
- Participants will listen to several children's poems.
- Participants will create a short poem.

Planning for Literacy Booster Meeting

Several weeks in advance

❑ Select date and reserve a room with adequate space. Internet access is recommended but not required.

❑ Arrange for equipment: a long table to be placed at the front of room on which to display children's books; chairs; podium; computer, projector, and screen.

❑ Review PowerPoint presentation (optional).

❑ Announce to faculty and staff; solicit support, participation, and assistance.

❑ Send home inviting announcement of Literacy Booster Meeting Session 2 listing all pertinent details including date, time, and purpose of meeting.

❑ Arrange for publicity via the school website and calendar, classroom calendars, announcements, and school parent organization communications.

❑ As event draws near, distribute registration form. Prominently list response date to facilitate preparation of the room and ensure ample copies and materials. If childcare or transportation will be provided, give details. (See sample.)

❑ Arrange for a childcare room; solicit volunteers to staff (optional).

One week in advance

❑ Send reminder to families.

❑ Confirm room.

❑ Confirm childcare and transportation arrangements, if applicable.

❑ Arrange for refreshments.

❑ Make copies of Resource Packet. Note: It may be helpful to reproduce the "Read-Aloud Tips" page from the Session 1 Resource Packet and have it available, or place it in the Session 3 packet for participants who did not attend the previous sessions.

❑ Gather and become familiar with children's books.

❑ Practice read-aloud.

❑ Write your birthday month poem. (See instructions in meeting plan.)

❑ Become familiar with featured websites.

The day of the event

❑ Set up room (projector, screen, materials to disseminate, pens or pencils).

❑ Display children's books on a large table at the front of the room.

❑ Arrange chairs for easy viewing of screen and to facilitate discussion.

❑ Gather refreshments for break (optional).

❑ Check on childcare and transportation arrangements, if provided.

Leading the Literacy Booster Meeting

○ Warmly and enthusiastically greet parents/caregivers as they arrive. Encourage browsing of books on display.

○ 5 minutes: **Begin promptly** with a welcome, an explanation of the goals for the event (see above), and a reminder to silence cell phones. Circulate attendance sheet. Review location of restrooms and fire/emergency exit details.

○ 10 minutes: **Overview of Meeting**

• Introduce staff present at the meeting.

• Ask if there are any questions related to the previous session. Encourage participants to ask questions and share comments pertinent to the topic throughout the meeting.

• Review schedule for the meeting.

• State goals for the meeting (see above). **(PP)**

• Ask parents/caregivers to introduce themselves, state the ages of their children, and tell why they signed up for/what they hope to gain from this final Literacy Booster Meeting focusing on reading aloud. **(PP)** Note responses briefly on chart paper/whiteboard.

• Draw attention to children's poetry books on display.

• Distribute Resource Packet and briefly overview contents.

○ 10 minutes: **Recap Reading Aloud Experiences with Older Children**

• Ask participants to tell about read-aloud experiences with their older children that took place as a result of the second Read-Aloud Literacy Booster Meeting. Solicit details, such as ages of children, how often they read aloud, how long read-alouds took, and types or titles of books.

• Comment positively; reinforce salient points; encourage brief discussion of what parents/caregivers found of value in the experiences. Be enthusiastic; reinforce positive comments.

• Review read-aloud tips and discuss how participants followed them. Note: It may be helpful to reproduce the "Read-Aloud Tips" page and have it available for participants who were not in attendance at the previous sessions, or add it to the Session 3 packet.

○ 10 minutes: **Reading Aloud Here, There, and Every-which-where!**

• Refer to the pages in the Resource Packet that offer suggestions for how to bolster literacy every day. Discuss.

• Tell participants: We've covered reading aloud to our children from birth through the teen years in the past two sessions in this series. From our discussions I sense you are working toward making reading aloud a family habit. Your children will treasure and benefit from this. We've also looked at a variety of ways to snag reading opportunities here, there, and every-which-where! I want to offer one more type of reading aloud that's fast, easy, and entertaining, and it offers tremendous benefits to your children. We're going to explore POETRY!

○ 15 minutes: **Introduction to Poetry**
  • Ask the following questions:
    • When you hear the word *poetry* what comes to mind? Participants may admit to feeling uncomfortable, unfamiliar with, or alienated from poetry for a variety of reasons. Jot responses on chart paper/whiteboard. Encourage discussion.
    • Can you recall a favorite nursery rhyme? Care to recite?
    • Why do we love and remember nursery rhymes?
  • Read aloud a nursery rhyme from the packet. Be expressive! Model effective read-aloud behaviors.
  • After you read the poem, ask:
    ▪ Are you familiar with this nursery rhyme?
    ▪ Do you like this poem? Why?
    ▪ What are some features of this nursery rhyme?
    ▪ What did you notice I did as I read this poem?
    ▪ Do you read or recite nursery rhymes to your young ones?
  • Discuss the merits of nursery rhymes.
    ▪ Nursery rhymes introduce very young children to language, word play, rhythm, and rhyme.
    ▪ Repetition of rhymes help children learn how language works.
    ▪ Hearing rhymes and learning rhymes builds memory capabilities.
    ▪ Nursery rhymes connect us—whether it's a group of children or a group of children and adults.
    ▪ Nursery rhymes are snappy fun!
    ▪ Nursery rhymes are referred to in ads, TV programs, books, cartoons, and films. Those who don't know nursery rhymes are shortchanged in conversations, discussions, and in understanding references in films, books, and other media.

    ▪ Note nursery rhyme collections listed in the Resource Packet.

  • Read aloud one of the general poems in the Resource Packet.
  • After reading the poem, discuss:
    ▪ Do you like this poem? Why?
    ▪ What do you notice about the poem?
    ▪ What did you notice I did as I read this poem?
    ▪ Do you see yourself reading poetry to your children?
  • Discuss the merits of poetry.
    ▪ Poetry encourages a love of language and words.
    ▪ Poetry increases vocabulary.

- Poetry is short and compact. It drives home a point or a message with few words. This can be appealing to children.
  - Reading poetry to your children is a quick, fun, literacy moment. All you need to get started is a few poems in your back pocket or a book of poems on a favorite subject.
- Note poetry collections listed in the Resource Packet.
- Encourage participants to try reading poetry to their children. Caution that it might take some getting used to, but like anything else, the more poems they read, the more comfortable they will be with the form, and the more enjoyment they—and their children—will get from poetry. Relax; feel the rhythm of the poem. Note the punctuation to get the flow right. Not all poems rhyme, but all poems have rhythm! Practice reading a poem aloud before you read it to your child. Listen for the rhythm.
  - 10 minutes: **Break**
    - Offer refreshments (optional).
    - Encourage participants to browse children's poetry books.
  - 10 minutes: **Poetry Activity**
    - Tell participants that though they may not realize it, they all have what it takes to be a poet.
    - Read aloud "August" by Paul B. Janeczko, from *Here's a Little Poem: A Very First Book of Poetry*, collected by Jane Yolen and Andrew Fusek Peters, and illustrated by Polly Dunbar.
    - Ask participants to turn to the notes page.
    - Direct participants to write a 2–3 line poem about the month in which they were born in the spirit of the poem just read to them. Their poem does not have to rhyme, but they will want to include sensory images—words that appeal to one or more of the senses.
    - Allow 5 minutes for participants to create their poems.
    - Beginning with January, ask volunteers to read their poems. When it comes to your birthday month, read your poem!
    - Keep it fun as volunteers read their poems. Consider handing out wrapped candy or colorful pencils to those who read their poems!
  - 10 minutes: **Websites Focusing on Poetry for Children**
    - Ask participants to turn to the page in the Resource Packet that lists poetry websites for children.
    - Briefly introduce as many sites as time allows. If Internet access is available, open link and give an overview of the site and its purpose and value. Navigate through the site, highlighting points of interest. Solicit comments; encourage discussion.
  - 10 minutes: **Close the session**
    - Review goals of meeting. Recap strategies and reinforce the value of reading aloud to children. (**PP**)

- Ask: What is one thing you will take away from this meeting?
- Discuss: Do you see yourself reading poetry to your children?
- Encourage parents/caregivers to read a fun poem to their children tonight. Suggestions appear in the handout. Read one to the group if time allows.
- Ask participants to complete a short evaluation of the meeting in order to offer valuable feedback for future meetings. (See Appendix for example.)
- Thank participants for attending.
- Conclude meeting on time.

Resource Packet for Why Should I Read to My Child? Session 3: Reading Together Here, There, and Every-Which-Where! can be found on the following pages. See also related Take-Home TipSheets in Chapter 12. TipSheets in color and in Spanish can be found in eResources online.

Gene Bradbury. Photograph used with permission.

Join us for our final session revealing surefire ways to help our children become star students and lifelong readers!

Why Should I Read to My Child?
Session 3

Reading Here, There, and Every-Which-Where!

_____

Date and time

_____

Place

Please return registration form by

_____

Date

Yes, I/we will attend **Why Should I Read to My Child? Session 3**

Parent(s)/Caregiver(s) _____ _____

Teacher _____ Room _____

Number of adults attending _____

Session 3
Parent/Caregiver
Resource Packet

Reading Here, There, and Every-Which-Where!

Make your Home Book-Bountiful!

Place Books in

> ➤ **B**askets
> ➤ **B**edrooms
> ➤ **B**athrooms
> ➤ **B**ackpacks
> ➤ **B**ack seats
> ➤ **B**irthday gift bags!

Don't forget Magazines
Newspapers and

 e-readers count, too!

Expand the Experience

➤ **Read** road signs and billboards while traveling in the car.

➤ **Read** a poem while your child brushes his teeth, packs his backpack, or zips up his jacket before heading for the bus.

➤ Encourage family and friends to **read** a book or newspaper article with your child.

➤ Have children **read** TV listings to find favorite shows.

➤ Ask your child to **read** aloud directions for the board game your family plans to play.

➤ Ask your child to **read** greeting cards when they arrive in the mail.

➤ Suggest that your child read cereal boxes and other food packages, front and back. Discuss nutritional information. Do the math on calories and servings.

➤ Ask for help making meals. Have your child **read** the recipe!

➤ Encourage your child to **read** catalog descriptions and ads to compare prices of products and models when selecting an item they need or want.

➤ Write and **read** your own books or lyrics to songs!

Ways to Spark Reading Every-Which-Way!

➤ Create a colorful alphabet book based on family members, summer vacation, neighborhood, pets, a day at the zoo, or a favorite activity or sport.

➤ Form a neighborhood or after-school book club with other parents/caregivers and children of similar ages. Schedule periodic meetings. Have fun discussing books children choose to read.

➤ Read the book before you see the movie, and then talk about the differences between them.

➤ Read and then write a mystery story, a ghost story, a fantasy, or a poem!

➤ Read billboards to your preschooler.

➤ Discuss messages behind billboards and ads with your preteen or teen.

➤ Read the first chapter of a really good adventure story and then leave the book on your middle grader's night stand (or on top of a pile of favorite t-shirts on the floor by the closet)!

➤ Read poetry. Focus on your child's favorite activities, dreaded chores, or everyday routines. Choose funny poems, too!

➤ Visit favorite authors' websites. Illustrators' websites are typically visual treats. **Always monitor your child's use of the Internet.**

➤ Get caught reading. Your kids look up to you—you're a role model!

Nursery Rhymes

Jack Sprat could eat no fat,
His wife could eat no lean;
And so between them both,
They licked the platter clean.

Jack and Jill
Went up the hill,
To fetch a pail of water;
Jack fell down
And broke his crown,
And Jill came tumbling after.

Billy boy blue, come blow me your horn,
The sheep's in the meadow, the cow's in the corn;
Is that the way you mind your sheep,
Under the haycock fast asleep!

Little Miss Muffet,
Sat on a tuffet,
Eating some curds and whey;
There came a great spider,
And sat down beside her,
And frightened Miss Muffet away.

A Fun Poem to Share with Your Kids Today!

"The City Mouse and the Country Mouse"
by Jean de La Fontaine

A City Mouse, with ways polite,
A Country Mouse invited
To sup with him and spend the night.
Said Country Mouse: "De—lighted!"
In truth it proved a royal treat,
With everything that's good to eat.

Alas! When they had just begun
To gobble their dinner,
A knock was heard that made them run.
The City Mouse seemed thinner.
And as they scampered and turned tail,
He saw the Country Mouse grow pale.

The knocking ceased. A false alarm!
The City Mouse grew braver.
"Come back!" he cried. "No, no! The farm,
Where I'll not quake or quaver,
Suits me," replied the Country Mouse.
"You're welcome to your city house."

Next, find a copy of a children's book with this title in the library and read that tomorrow. Or, go online for readings of the story and tons of fun activities!

Poetry
Mini Read-Alouds/Maxi Benefits for Ages 3–7

Nursery Rhymes

- ❖ *Marguerite De Angeli's Book of Nursery and Mother Goose Rhymes*.
- ❖ *Mother Goose's Little Treasures*, collected by Iona Opie, illustrated by Rosemary Wells.
- ❖ *Over the Candlestick: Classic Nursery Rhymes and the Real Stories Behind Them*, collected by Michael G. Montgomery and Wayne Montgomery, illustrated by Michael G. Montgomery.
- ❖ *A Pocketful of Posies: A Treasury of Nursery Rhymes*, illustrated by Salley Mavor.
- ❖ *The Real Mother Goose*, illustrated by Blanche Fisher Wright.
- ❖ *Richard Scarry's Best Mother Goose Ever*.
- ❖ *Tomie de Paola's Mother Goose*, collected and illustrated by Tomie de Paola.

General

- ❖ *Animals, Animals*, edited and illustrated by Eric Carle.
- ❖ *Animal Crackers: A Delectable Collection of Pictures, Poems, and Lullabies for the Very Young*, selected and illustrated by Jane Dyer.
- ❖ *The Bill Martin Jr. Big Book of Poetry*, edited by Bill Martin Jr. with Michael Sampson.
- ❖ *Blackberry Ink*, by Eve Merriam, illustrated by Hans Wilhelm.
- ❖ *Calendar*, by Myra Cohn Livingston, illustrated by Will Hillenbrand.
- ❖ *A Child's Calendar*, by John Updike, illustrated by Trina Schart Hyman.
- ❖ *A Child's Garden of Verses*, by Robert Louis Stevenson.
- ❖ *The Everything Book*, by Denise Fleming.
- ❖ *A Family of Poems: My Favorite Poetry for Children*, collected by Caroline Kennedy, illustrated by Jon J. Muth.
- ❖ *Here's a Little Poem: A Very First Book of Poetry*, collected by Jane Yolen and Andrew Fusek Peters, illustrated by Polly Dunbar.
- ❖ *Holiday Stew*, by Jenny Whitehead.
- ❖ *I Invited a Dragon to Dinner and Other Poems to Make You Laugh Out Loud*, illustrated by Chris L. Demarest.
- ❖ *I Like Being Me: Poems for Children about Feeling Special, Appreciating Others, and Getting Along*, by Judy Lalli, photographs by Douglas L. Mason-Fry.
- ❖ *The Ice Cream Store*, by Dennis Lee, illustrated by David McPhail.

❖ *Little Dog Poems*, by Kristine O'Connell George, illustrated by June Otani.
❖ *Little Poems for Tiny Ears*, by Lin Oliver, illustrated by Tomie dePaola.
❖ *One Big Rain: Poems for Rainy Days*, compiled by Rita Gray, illustrated by Ryan O'Rourke.
❖ *Read-Aloud Rhymes for the Very Young*, selected by Jack Prelutsky, illustrated by Marc Brown.
❖ *The Reason for the Pelican*, by John Ciardi, illustrated by Dominic Catalano.
❖ *Rufus and Friends Rhyme Time: Traditional Poems Extended and Illustrated*, by Iza Trapani.
❖ *Seven Little Rabbits*, by John Becker, illustrated by Barbara Cooney.
❖ *Sing a Song of Popcorn, Every Child's Book of Poems*, selected by Beatrice Schenk de Regniers, Eva Moore, Mary Michaels White, and Jan Carr; illustrated by nine Caldecott Medal artists.
❖ *Talking Like the Rain: A Read-to-me Book of Poems*, selected by X. J. Kennedy and Dorothy M. Kennedy, illustrated by Jane Dyer.
❖ *You Know Who*, poems by John Ciardi, illustrated by Edward Gorey.

Seasonal

Spring
❖ *Easter Buds Are Springing: Poems for Easter*, selected by Lee Bennett Hopkins, illustrated by Tomie de Paola.
❖ *Puddle Wonderful Poems to Welcome Spring*, selected by Bobbi Katz, illustrated by Mary Morgan.

Summer
❖ *Anna's Summer Songs*, by Mary Q. Steele, illustrated by Lena Anderson.
❖ *Beat the Drum Independence Day Has Come: Poems for the Fourth of July*, selected by Lee Bennett Hopkins, illustrated by Tomie de Paola.
❖ *The Ice Cream Store*, poems by Dennis Lee, illustrated by David McPhail.
❖ *Summersaults*, by Douglas Florian.

Fall
❖ *Autumnblings*, by Douglas Florian.
❖ *Ghosts and Goose Bumps: Poems to Chill Your Bones*, selected by Bobbi Katz, illustrated by Deborah Kogan Ray.
❖ *Halloween ABC*, by Eve Merriam, illustrated by Lane Smith.
❖ *It's Halloween*, by Jack Prelutsky, illustrated by Marylin Hafner.
❖ *It's Thanksgiving*, by Jack Prelutsky, illustrated by Marylin Hafner.

Winter
❖ *It's Christmas*, by Jack Prelutsky, illustrated by Marylin Hafner.
❖ *Little Tree*, by e.e. cummings, illustrated by Deborah Kogan Ray.
❖ *Winter Poems*, selected by Barbara Rogasky, illustrated by Trina Schart Hyman.

Poetry
Mini Read-Alouds/ Maxi Benefits for Ages 8–11

❖ *Another Jar of Tiny Stars*, edited by Bernice E. Cullinan and Deborah Wooten.

❖ *Dear World*, by Takayo Noda.

❖ *Dirty Laundry Pile: Poems in Different Voices*, selected by Paul B. Janeczko, illustrated by Melissa Sweet.

❖ *The Fastest Game on Two Feet and Other Poems about How Sports Began*, by Alice Low, illustrated by John O'Brien.

❖ *Forest Has a Song*, by Amy Ludwig VanDerwater, illustrated by Robin Gourley.

❖ *Heroes and She-Roes: Poems of Amazing and Everyday Heroes*, by J. Patrick Lewis, illustrated by Jim Cooke.

❖ *Joyful Noise: Poems for Two Voices*, by Paul Fleischman, illustrated by Eric Beddows.

❖ *Lemonade and Other Poems Squeezed from a Single Word*, by Bob Raczka, illustrated by Nancy Doniger.

❖ *Mama Says: A Book of Love for Mothers and Sons*, by Rob D. Walker, illustrated by Leo and Diane Dillon.

❖ *Never Forgotten*, by Patricia C. McKissack, illustrated by Leo and Diane Dillon.

❖ *Not a Copper Penny in Me House: Poems from the Caribbean*, by Monica Gunning, illustrated by Frané Lessac.

❖ *The Snack Smasher and Other Reasons Why It's Not My Fault*, by Andrea Perry, illustrated by Alan Snow.

❖ *Squeeze: Poems from a Juicy Universe*, by Heidi Mordhorst, photographs by Jesse Torrey.

❖ *Steady Hands: Poems about Work*, by Tracie Vaughn Zimmer, illustrated by Megan Halsey and Sean Addy.

❖ *Swirl by Swirl: Spirals in Nature*, by Joyce Sidman, illustrated by Beth Krommes.

❖ *The Underwear Salesman and Other Jobs for Better or Verse*, by J. Patrick Lewis, illustrated by Serge Bloch.

❖ *Yes! We Are Latinos*, by Alma Flor Ada and F. Isabel Campoy, illustrated by David Diaz.

Literacy Is Power!

Poetry Websites to Check Out!

❖ http://jackprelutsky.com/ *The website of Jack Prelutsky, named the first U.S. Children's Poet Laureate in 2006.*

❖ www.jpatricklewis.com/ *The website of J. Patrick Lewis, U.S. Children's Poet Laureate, 2011–2013.*

❖ www.poetry4kids.com/ *The website of Ken Nesbitt, U.S. Children's Poet Laureate.*

❖ www.personal.umich.edu/~pfa/dreamhouse/nursery/rhymesABC.html *This website offers an alphabetical list of Mother Goose nursery rhymes.*

❖ www.poets.org/poetsorg/text/poems-kids *Find a list of poems kids are sure to like on the site of the Academy of American Poets.*

❖ www.poemfarm.amylv.com/ *Chock-full, engaging, fun site of Amy Ludwig VanDerwater.*

❖ www.janetwong.com/ *Click on the microphone to the far left on the home page to hear Janet S. Wong recite her poems.*

❖ www.rebeccakaidotlich.com/writing/tips/tips01.html *Find simple tips for young poets on Rebecca Kai Dotlich's website.*

❖ www.kristinegeorge.com/ *A comprehensive site; don't miss the entertaining Kids! page or the parents' page.*

❖ www.poetryguy.com/ *Jazzy site of Ted Scheu (rhymes with guy).*

❖ www.gigglepoetry.com/ *Find poetry fun at the website of Meadowbrook Press, the publisher of many humorous poetry books for children.*

❖ www.pbs.org/parents/education/bookfinder/celebrating-poetry/ *PBS Parents' Page cites the benefits of poetry for children, offers tips for broadening kids' interest in poetry, and lists recommended poetry books for children.*

Notes

You will never be alone with a poet in your pocket.

—John Adams

Part IV

Additional Parent/ Caregiver Literacy Booster Meetings and Family Literacy Events

CHAPTER 7

Organize It!
And Avoid Homework Hassles

Striving to become more organized regularly shows up in lists of New Year's resolutions; magazine articles abound with creative ideas. A person who has a sense of organization is often less stressed, more productive, and produces higher quality work (Mellor 2013). Parents/caregivers can assist their children in developing organizational skills that will be of benefit for many years to come. Rather than rigid, demanding rules that must be followed, organization and structure offer a sense of control over tasks that must be tackled. In helping children become more organized, we provide them with tools to become better students (Bakunas and Holley 2001). Not only will children be more productive at school, but organizational skills may reduce friction when it comes to completing homework.

There is conflicting research on the value of homework. It has been shown that having students complete assignments at home has little effect on academic achievement (Kraklovec and Buell 2001; Bennett and Kalish 2006; Chen and Stevenson 1989). Other studies demonstrate definite academic gains (Alleman and Brophy 1991; Xu and Corno 1998; Warton 2001). Research shows benefits other than achievement associated with completing homework, such as developing study skills, a sense of responsibility, task management, and increased motivation (Cooper et al. 2001). There have been many discussions on the length and types of assignments that may be beneficial and the characteristics of students who may benefit. Findings suggest broad guidelines. Early elementary students whose parents/caregivers help them organize and complete homework benefit by developing routines, structure, and study skills (Cooper et al. 2006). Older students, usually with less parental guidance, demonstrate increased academic gains when they regularly study and complete homework (Bembenutty 2011).

When children first enter school, a routine for reading at home on a daily basis ought to be established if not already in place. Likewise, a system for completing homework ought to be consistent. Parents/caregivers can be instrumental in helping children gain a positive outlook toward homework and in providing guidance in developing organizational skills that will last a lifetime. As children grow older, they should gradually take on responsibility for homework, and parents/caregivers should strive to become less involved in their children's assignments.

Nonetheless, parents/caregivers continue to influence their children's organization skills in many ways (Bakunas and Holley 2001). This Literacy Booster Meeting will help equip parents/caregivers with skills, strategies, and tools they can use to aid students in adapting to the demands of school work as they grow from early learner to middle grade student.

Organize It! Helping Your Child Develop Strategies for Success with Homework

Grade Levels: K–5

Time: 1.5 hours

Supplies
- Large room with several tables and enough chairs to seat all comfortably
- Chart paper/whiteboard and markers
- Copies of Resource Packet
- Read-aloud book
- Document reader, opaque projector, or some other means of sharing read-aloud book
- Pencils/pens
- Small note paper or sticky notes
- Calendar, agenda, week-in-review page (enlarged or drawn on board)
- Box of supplies (See Parent/Caregiver Checklist in Resource Packet)
- Light refreshments (optional)

Goals
- Participants will learn how organization can help their children be more effective students.
- Participants will become familiar with tools and techniques that aid in developing organizational skills.
- Participants will become familiar with positive strategies for working with their children.
- Participants will be encouraged to ask questions to clarify what they have learned so they can implement the tools, techniques, and strategies in the home.

Literacy Booster Meeting Planning

Several weeks in advance
- ❑ Select date, reserve room, and arrange childcare and transportation, if provided.
- ❑ Arrange for publicity via the school website, classroom calendars, announcements, and the school parent organization.

❑ As event draws near, send an invitation to all families. Include a registration form to be returned to enable preparation of the room and ensure ample copies and materials. (See Resource Packet)

❑ Gather an alarm clock, timer, and box of supplies (See Resource Packet.)

One week in advance
❑ Send reminder to families.

❑ Confirm room and childcare arrangements.

❑ Make copies of Resource Packet.

The day of the event
❑ Set up the room and lay out all materials.

❑ Display recommended children's books.

❑ As parents/caregivers arrive, greet them, distribute packets, and invite them to be seated.

Leading the Literacy Booster Meeting

○ 5 minutes: **Start promptly** with a warm welcome, introduction of all staff present, a reminder to silence all cell phones, and an explanation of the goals for the event. Circulate the attendance sheet. Review location of restrooms and fire/emergency exit details.

○ **Talking Points**
- We can all learn to be better organized.
- There are many products that help us to become more organized.
- There are also many strategies and tools that help students become better organized.
- Helping your children become more organized increases their productivity and responsibility.
- Homework sometimes can be a battle. A sense of organization can decrease stress in the home.

○ 10 minutes: **Parent/caregiver input**
- Ask parents/caregivers to think about what issues and questions they have regarding homework and organizational skills. Have note paper handy for participants to jot down thoughts if they are reticent to speak. Be an active listener. Note comments on chart paper/whiteboard. Refer to the list of comments during the meeting to assure participants that their concerns are being addressed.
- Explain that you will try to address all questions and concerns within the time constraints. Highlight those you cannot address, and indicate that you will communicate a response in another meeting or a future communication.

○ 10 minutes: **Read aloud** *Peanut Butter and Homework Sandwiches*, by Lisa Broadie Cook, or *The Worst Day of My Life Ever!*, by Julia Cook. (See list of Recommended Read-Alouds for additional titles.)

○ 20 minutes: **Part I Time Organization Presentation**

○ **Talking Points**

• Invest in two tools: an alarm clock and a timer. Children develop independence by learning to set a clock and wake up when it rings. Analog clocks give children a visual sense of time. Students can see how much time has gone by without getting out of bed. An analog clock helps develop a sense of time that is not fostered by digital clocks.

• A kitchen timer can be invaluable for building in breaks during a homework period, defining playtime, or helping children develop a sense of how much time has passed.

• As soon as your child is old enough, buy a personal calendar as a gift. Find one that matches your child's interest. Keep the calendar where you can both easily access it. Ask: How can we use this with younger children? Elicit responses. Suggestions:

  ▪ We can help them write in important dates or use stickers.

  ▪ We can help them count down the days until a specific event takes place.

  ▪ We can use the calendar to write down the dates assignments are due.

• Ask: How can we use a calendar with older students? Elicit responses. Suggestions:

  ▪ Each month the child can be encouraged to write in important dates, such as birthdays, music lessons, and after-school events. Do not fill in the entire year all at once. Schedules change and the task can seem overwhelming.

  ▪ Help the child write in test dates. Schedule study times in the days leading up to the test. When longer term projects are due, help the child break the project into smaller, more manageable units and block off time for completion of those steps. For example, when a book report is due, decide a date by which the child needs to have completed reading the book. Mark it on the calendar. Next, divide up the pages and mark the calendar with the page goal for each night. Designate dates and times for completing the rough draft, revisions, and final report.

  ▪ By teaching students how to break large tasks into a series of smaller ones, we help them learn that they can accomplish more work and of higher quality by spreading the tasks out, rather than trying to do all the work the night before it is due.

• Look at the Week-at-a-Glance page

  ▪ Take a few minutes each weekend to help your child look ahead to the events of the upcoming week. Filling in the time they get home from school, sports practices, instrument practice, and family events will help them (and you) plan and schedule.

  ▪ Refer to the calendar and transfer important information to this weekly schedule. Some schools provide an agenda for older students. If we help children see this as a useful tool in organizing their day-to-day tasks, they will not forget to use it.

  ▪ Let's fill out a practice Week-at-a-Glance

    ▪ Start with Sunday. What are your family routines? If you attend a religious service, visit family, or have a family dinner, mark down established routines and designate times.

- Block homework/study/reading time. Even if a child has no homework assigned on a weekend, the designated block should be used for reading, reviewing notes, working on long-range projects, or studying for tests.
- Now let's look at the weekdays. Write in the time your child gets home from school, dinner, sports, and other commitments.
- Designate time for homework tasks **and** time to relax and play. It is important for children to see they have unscheduled time to use as they please.
- Talk with your child about designating homework time. Each child is different. Some like to come home and get the work out of the way immediately. Some need to play or rest after sitting in a classroom all day in order to be more effective when completing homework. Honor your child's preference.
- A Homework Contract is included in the Resource Packet. Ask your child for input into the conditions and consequences. Parent/caregiver and child should negotiate this agreement, in writing, and sign it. Parents/caregivers need to enforce the consequences when homework is not completed according to the agreement. Being steadfast initially reaps benefits later when you can simply refer to the signed contract if an issue arises.
- Be sure to schedule time for choosing clothing, making lunches, packing backpacks, bedtime rituals, and don't forget recreational reading.

○ 10 minutes: **Break**
  - Give participants a few minutes to stretch and converse with each other. Serve refreshments (optional).

○ 15 minutes: **Part II Space Management**
  - Have parents/caregivers review the Parent/Caregiver Checklist. Request that they check off things they already have or do at home. Ask them to identify one or two things they would like to change.
    - An organized environment will help children understand that completing schoolwork is serious business, an important part of their day, and a priority for the family.
  - Children need a place to work and study.
    - It may be a desk in their room, the kitchen table, or any area that is comfortable to spread out school materials.
    - Some children like to work in the kitchen while a parent/caregiver is preparing supper. Just beware of distractions wherever the child chooses to work.
    - Students should work free from electronic distractions. It is beneficial to begin a policy early in the school career of no cell phones, music devices, or tablets.
    - Although many teens and tweens report that they cannot study without music, research shows that removing distractions enables the brain to focus on the task at hand.
    - For online safety, students should be within view of a parent/caregiver when using the computer.

- Good lighting is a necessity. Bright, fluorescent lighting can cause eye fatigue. Opt for soft white, non-glare light bulbs.
- Keep school supplies in a specified drawer or box. Help your child develop the habit of putting things back where they belong so time is not wasted searching for materials.
- Designate a specific place for school-related items, such as backpacks, library books, and school notices. This will save time when children are getting ready for school.

○ 15 minutes: **Homework Tips**
- Develop routine and structure with children in the early school years. Children in the primary grades often need guidance when completing homework. Help them develop organizational skills by providing support. Sit with them. Let them independently complete as much of the work as possible. Give positive reinforcement when they complete work independently.
- By the end of elementary school, students should be doing most work independently, though they may still benefit from help studying for tests or reviewing written work.
- Consider strategies for children who avoid doing assignments, refuse to complete homework, or create stressful situations related to homework.
  - Schedule a conference with the teacher.
  - Ask about expectations. Should homework be completed independently? How much time should it take? Where are assignments listed?
  - If the teacher feels the student is capable of completing the work independently, consider using the Homework Contract.
  - When starting homework, ask your child to explain the assignment. If your child cannot do this, ask him or her to re-read the directions or assignment aloud. Explain, if necessary.
  - Once you feel the student has an idea of what is expected, leave the student to work alone for a while.
  - Check periodically; offer encouragement. Avoid doing your child's work. This pattern is difficult to break. A little "tough love" goes a long way!
  - If a student sits for hours doing homework but seldom completes it, set a timer for a reasonable length of time. When the timer goes off, have your student put the assignment in the backpack.
  - The next day, the student must explain why the assignment is not done. If it is truly a case of not having the skills to do the assignment, the teacher should be made aware of this so additional instruction can be provided. If the student simply balks at completing the work, the fact that he or she must discuss this with the teacher may change the work ethic.
- Included in the Resource Packet are several graphic organizers, which may be beneficial to students when completing assignments. An explanation and suggestions for their use are provided. The Common Core State Standards require students to "delineate and evaluate the argument and specific claims in a text, including the

validity of the reasoning as well as the relevance and sufficiency of the evidence" (CCSS.ELA-Literacy.CCRA.R.8). Using graphic organizers when completing homework can enhance understanding and increase learning.

- ○ 5 minutes: **Closing the Literacy Booster Meeting**
  - Ask if there are any questions.
  - Review the list on the chart paper/whiteboard. Have all questions/concerns been addressed? If not, determine if they can be answered quickly or if they can be addressed through another meeting or a future communication.
  - Optional: Raffling off a timer, alarm clock, or calendar would be a fun conclusion to the meeting. Thank volunteers and participants for attending.
  - Transfer items on chart paper/whiteboard onto a follow-up sheet that can be sent home or included in a school newsletter.
  - Ask participants to complete a brief evaluation of the event in order to offer valuable feedback for future events. (See Appendix for an example of an evaluation form.)

Bibliography

Alleman, Janet and Jere E. Brophy, *Reconceptualizing Homework as Out-of-the-School Learning Opportunities* (Occasional Paper No. 135). East Lansing, MI: Michigan State University, Institute for Research in Teaching, May 1991.

Bakunas, Boris and William Holley, "Teaching Organizational Skills," *The Clearing House: A Journal of Educational Strategies, Issues and Ideas* 74, no. 3 (2001): 151–154, doi: 10.1080/00098650109599182

Bembenutty, Hefer, "The First Word: Homework's Theory, Research and Practice," *Journal of Advanced Academics* 22, no. 2 (February 2011): 185–193, doi: 10.1177/1932202x1102200201

Bennett, Sara and Nancy Kalish, *The Case Against Homework: How Homework Is Hurting Children and What Parents Can Do About It*. New York: Three Rivers Press, 2006.

Chen, Chuansheng and Harold W. Stevenson, "Homework: A Cross-cultural Examination," *Child Development* 60, no. 3 (June 1989): 551–56, doi:10.1111/j.1467-8624.1989.tb02736.x

Common Core State Standards, English Language Arts, College and Career Readiness Anchor Standards for Reading, Standard 8, www.corestandards.org/ELA-Literacy/

Cooper, Harris, Jorgianne Civey Robinson, and Erika A. Patall, "Does Homework Improve Academic Achievement? A Synthesis of Research, 1987–2003," *Review of Educational Research* 76, no. 1 (Spring 2006): 1–62, doi:10.3102/00346543076001001

Cooper, Harris, Kristina Jackson, Barbara Nye, and James J. Lindsay, "A Model of Homework's Influence on the Performance of Elementary School Students," *Journal of Experimental Education* 69, no. 2 (Winter 2001): 181–199, doi:10.1080/00220970109600655

Horsley, Mike and Richard Walker, *Reforming Homework: Practices, Learning and Policies*. Melbourne: Palgrave Macmillan, 2012.

Kraklovec, Etta and John Buell, *The End of Homework: How Homework Disrupts Families, Overburdens Children, and Limits Learning*. Boston: Beacon Press, August 2001.

Mellor, Nathan, "Reduce Stress by Being Organized," *Character First the Magazine*, accessed August 20, 2014, http://cfthemagazine.com/2013-01/reduce-stress-by-being-organized/

Warton, Pamela M., "The Forgotten Voice in Homework: Views of Students," *Educational Psychologist* 36, no. 3 (January 2001): 155–165, doi:10.1207/S15326985EP3603_2

Xu, Jianzhong and Lyn Corno, "Case Studies of Families Doing Third-grade Homework," *Teachers College Record* 100, no. 2 (Winter 1998): 403–436.

Resource Packet for Organize It! And Avoid Homework Hassles can be found on the following pages. See also related Take-Home TipSheet in Chapter 12.

Do your children need to be more organized?
Looking for ways to avoid homework hassles?

Come join us for

Organize It!

Help Your Child Develop Strategies
for Success with Homework!

_____

Date and time

_____

Place

Please return registration form by

_____

Date

Yes, I/we will attend **Organize It!**

Parent(s)/Caregiver(s) _____

Teacher _____ Room _____

Number of adults attending _____

Organize It!
Parent/Caregiver
Resource Packet

Week-at-a-Glance   *Week of* _____

Sunday	Monday	Tuesday	Wednesday	Thursday	Friday	Saturday

Homework Contract

Student: I promise to complete my homework each day at the agreed upon time. If I have no homework, I will read or study during that time.

Time _____ Place _____

Parent/Caregiver: I promise to provide adequate time and a place to complete homework. I will offer support and encouragement, and will assist only if I believe it is absolutely necessary.

Student Signature _____ Date _____

Parent/Caregiver Signature _____ Date _____

Agreed Upon Consequences: _____

_____

_____

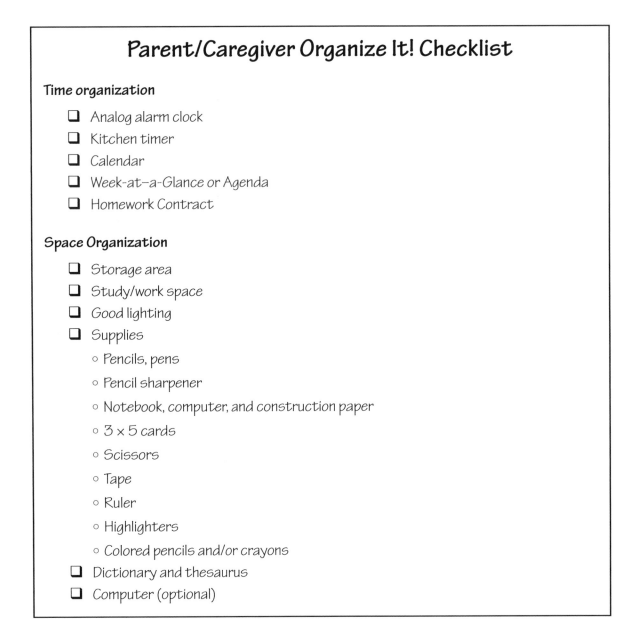

Parent/Caregiver Organize It! Checklist

Time organization

- ❏ Analog alarm clock
- ❏ Kitchen timer
- ❏ Calendar
- ❏ Week-at–a-Glance or Agenda
- ❏ Homework Contract

Space Organization

- ❏ Storage area
- ❏ Study/work space
- ❏ Good lighting
- ❏ Supplies
  - ○ Pencils, pens
  - ○ Pencil sharpener
  - ○ Notebook, computer, and construction paper
  - ○ 3 x 5 cards
  - ○ Scissors
  - ○ Tape
  - ○ Ruler
  - ○ Highlighters
  - ○ Colored pencils and/or crayons
- ❏ Dictionary and thesaurus
- ❏ Computer (optional)

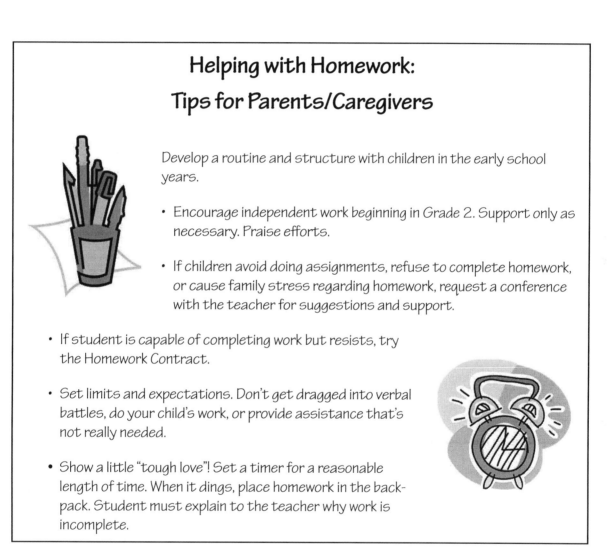

Helping with Homework:
Tips for Parents/Caregivers

Develop a routine and structure with children in the early school years.

- Encourage independent work beginning in Grade 2. Support only as necessary. Praise efforts.

- If children avoid doing assignments, refuse to complete homework, or cause family stress regarding homework, request a conference with the teacher for suggestions and support.

- If student is capable of completing work but resists, try the Homework Contract.

- Set limits and expectations. Don't get dragged into verbal battles, do your child's work, or provide assistance that's not really needed.

- Show a little "tough love"! Set a timer for a reasonable length of time. When it dings, place homework in the backpack. Student must explain to the teacher why work is incomplete.

Organizing is something you do before you do something, so that when you do it, it is not all mixed up.

—A. A. Milne, *creator of* Winnie the Pooh

Venn Diagram Graphic Organizer

Students use the Venn Diagram to compare and contrast two items, characters, or events. The subjects are placed on each line. Similarities are written in the overlapping middle section. Differences are written under the appropriate subject.

_____

Title

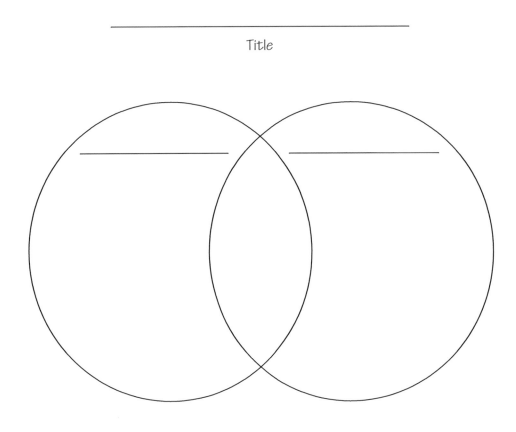

Time Line Graphic Organizer

After reading a text, students use the Time Line to place dates, times, and events in the order in which they occurred. This presents a visual, which enables the student to determine the sequence of events. There are several formats for Time Lines.

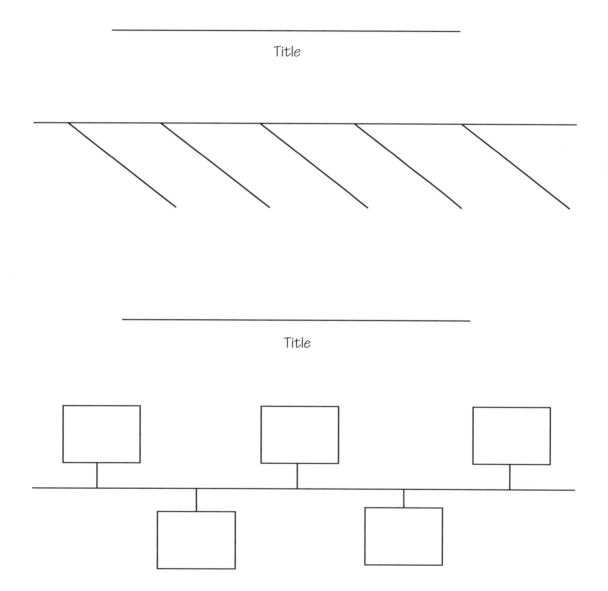

Title

Title

Flow Chart Graphic Organizer

Students use a Flow Chart to signal definite steps in a process. When steps are repeated, as in the life cycle, the cycle flow chart should be used.

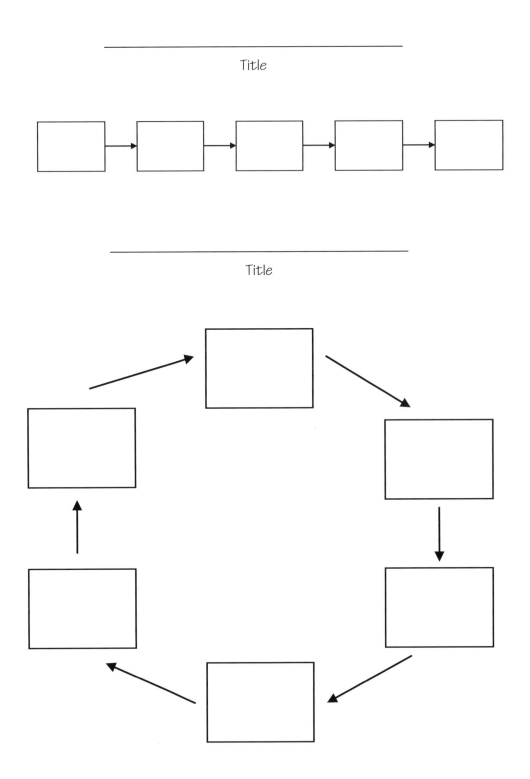

_____

Title

_____

Title

Cause and Effect Graphic Organizer

Students use the Cause and Effect organizer to describe the relationship between two actions or events. The left column describes the first action or event. The right column describes the reaction or result. Sometimes an action may have more than one resulting effect, as in the last set of boxes.

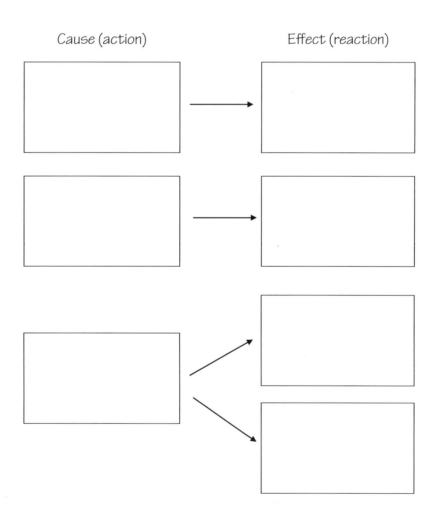

Cause (action)   Effect (reaction)

Narrative Arc Graphic Organizer

Students use the Narrative or Story Arc organizer to visualize the author's structure of a fiction (story) text.

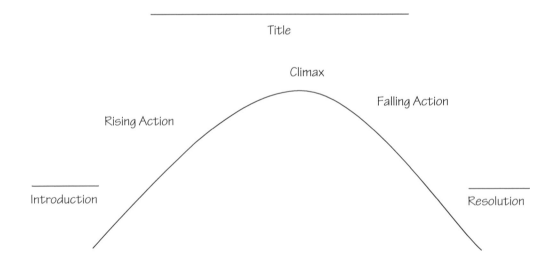

Recommended Read-Alouds

Amber Brown Wants Extra Credit, by Paula Danziger, illustrated by Tony Ross. Homework's late! Room's a mess! Mom troubles! Ages 7–10.

Dear Mr. Henshaw, by Beverly Cleary, illustrated by Paul O. Zelinsky. Sixth grader Leigh writes a letter to a favorite author as part of an assignment and a friendship grows, helping Leigh deal with difficult changes in his life. Ages 8–11.

The Girl Who Never Made Mistakes, by Mark Pett and Gary Rubinstein. See how perfect Beatrice copes with making her very first mistake. Ages 4–8.

Homework Hassles (Ready Freddy #3), by Abby Klein, illustrated by John McKinley. Freddy tries to get his homework in on time but runs into difficulties. Ages 5–8.

Measuring Penny, by Loreen Leedy. When Lisa has a homework assignment, her dog Penny comes in handy. Ages 6–8. See also: *It's Probably Penny*.

Messy Mark (First-Start Easy Reader), by Sharon Peters, illustrated by Irene Trivas. An easy reader about a boy who tries to neaten up. Ages 4–6.

Peanut Butter and Homework Sandwiches, by Lisa Broadie Cook, illustrated by Jack E. Davis. Martin has difficulties with his homework every day. He finally manages to make it fun and turns it in on time. Ages 5–8.

The Report Card, by Andrew Clements. Fifth grader Nora is smart, but she's fed up with tests and how they make some kids feel. When she purposely does poorly, Nora's in for more than she bargained for. Ages 8–11. See also: Jake Drake series for ages 7–9.

Sahara Special, by Esmé Raji Codell. Fifth grader Sahara doesn't do school work, but she loves to write—and that's only part of her story; a memorable novel. Ages 10–12.

The Worst Day of My Life Ever! (Best Me I Can Be series), by Julia Cook, illustrated by Kelsey De Weerd. RJ learns he must listen and follow directions. Ages 4–8. See also: Clementine series, by Sara Pennypacker (Ages 7–9) and Horrible Harry series, by Suzy Kline (Ages 6–8).

CHAPTER 8

Wrap It Up!
Gifts That Entertain and Support Learning

According to a survey by the American Research Group, Inc., on average Americans spend over $800 on holiday gifts per year (American Research Group, Inc. 2013). Surveys by the toy industry indicate that children in the United States receive an average of over $300 worth of toys annually (Statista 2011). In fact, it is estimated that U.S. children account for 3.7% of the total number of children across the world yet they possess 47% of all the toys and children's books (MacVean 2014). As educators, we can guide parents/caregivers in the purchase and use of toys that support and enrich learning, encourage the giving of books and other educational materials, and endeavor to convince parents/caregivers that the best gift they can give to their children doesn't cost a cent. It is the gift of time.

Building sets and blocks can increase children's visual-spatial, visual perception, and spatial visualization skills. These toys may lead to higher achievement in math and science (Caldera et al. 1999). Arts and crafts kits help develop eye-hand coordination and foster creativity. Art activities can sharpen the ability to observe one's surroundings in greater detail (Caldera et al. 1999). Crafts develop fine motor skills.

Board games can help develop deductive reasoning (Reid 2002); enhance social skills, such as how to be gracious winners and losers (Gobet et al. 2004); teach problem-solving skills; increase students' knowledge of cause and effect relationships; increase vocabulary; foster creativity; and sharpen motor planning (Sharp 2012). Such games enhance engagement, motivation, and discussion (Franklin 2003).

Simply having children build, create, or play by themselves will result in minimal impact on learning. However, when an adult becomes involved in an activity with a child, talks about the activity, shares thinking and reasoning, and encourages the child to do the same, the child learns from the adult and develops discussion and explanation skills. The Common Core State Standards in Mathematics not only ask students to compute accurately, but also require students to demonstrate the ability to "reason abstractly and quantitatively" and to "construct viable arguments and critique the reasoning of others" (CCSS.Math.Practice.MP2; CCSS.

Math.Practice.MP3). When a parent/caregiver talks with their child or makes up a story to provide context for a building activity, the child's motivation, enthusiasm, and spatial reasoning improve because the activity has more purpose (Casey et al. 2008). Assisting parents/caregivers in developing a habit of playing with their children and employing "think alouds" will increase vocabulary and language development in their children (Foster and Hund 2012).

Executive function is a term used to describe the set of skills people use in performing daily tasks. It encompasses inhibitory control, working memory, planning, organizing, and managing time and space. In a play setting, when a parent/caregiver truly engages with a child—rather than taking over and completing the activity—the parent/caregiver becomes more attuned to the child's abilities, strengths, and weaknesses; the parent/caregiver also becomes more aware of the mental processes of the child's executive functioning. The parent/caregiver is better equipped to provide scaffolding and guidance to help the child develop the skills necessary to be successful in a variety of similar tasks (Bernier et al. 2010).

In this Literacy Booster Event, parents/caregivers are offered suggestions for gift-giving and an opportunity to model guided problem-solving and verbal scaffolding that can enhance learning.

Wrap It Up! Great Gifts for Great Kids Literacy Booster Event

Grade Levels: Pre-K–5

Time: 1 hour

Supplies
- Large room for adults with tables and chairs to seat all comfortably
- Large room with tables for students
- Copies of Resource Packet
- Read-aloud book
- Document reader, opaque projector, or other means for sharing the read-aloud book
- Pencils
- A selection of age-appropriate board games
- A selection of various building blocks (Legos, wooden blocks, Lincoln Logs)
- A selection of craft materials (paper, markers, beads, glue, string, tape, scissors)
- Posters for student activity tables (See samples in eResources online.)
- Several board games, such as Connect Four, for parent/caregiver demonstration, or
- computer with Internet connection and projector
- Toy car and building blocks for parent/caregiver demonstration
- Purchased or computer-generated kid-friendly bookplates, one per child (See Resource Packet.)

- A selection of children's books for adults to browse (See Recommended Read-Alouds in Resource Packet.)
- Light refreshments (optional)

Goals
- Parents/caregivers will engage in activities that demonstrate that time is the best gift they can give their children.
- Parents/caregivers will become familiar with educational gift ideas and resources.
- Parents/caregivers will experience the educational value of games, building blocks, and crafts.
- Parents/caregivers will practice "think alouds" during activities.

Literacy Booster Event Planning

Several weeks in advance
- ❑ Select the date and reserve two large rooms.
- ❑ Recruit at least two volunteers to staff the student room.
- ❑ Arrange for publicity through the school website, calendar, classroom calendars, announcements, and the school parent organization.
- ❑ Arrange for childcare and transportation, if provided.
- ❑ Collect board games, building blocks, children's books, and craft materials. If staff lends materials, label them so they can be returned after the event.
- ❑ As event draws near, send an invitation to all families. Include a registration form to be returned to enable preparation of the room and ample materials. (See example in Resource Packet.)

One week in advance
- ❑ Confirm rooms, materials, and volunteers.
- ❑ Send reminder to families.
- ❑ Check on childcare and transportation arrangements, if provided.
- ❑ Make posters, bookmarks, and copies of Resource Packet.
- ❑ Practice the read-aloud. You are modeling the read-aloud behaviors you wish to foster in the participants.
- ❑ If using a computer with projector, go to www.agame.com/game/connect-four. Make sure you can access the Connect Four game. (See Resource Packet for additional websites.)

The day of the event
- ❑ Set up materials in the student room. Three separate stations are recommended: Games, Building Blocks, and Craft Zone. (See eResources online for examples of posters.)

❑ In parent/caregiver room, set up games or check computer connection and projector. Go to www.agame.com/game/connect-four. Make sure you can access the Connect Four game. If unsuccessful, use board game. Set up a display of children's books.

❑ Greet participants as they arrive. Invite students to explore the games and materials in students' room. Distribute Resource Packets to parents/caregivers and encourage them to peruse the books on display.

Leading the Literacy Booster Event

○ 5 minutes: **Start promptly**. Welcome everyone, introduce staff present, request all cell phones be silenced, and explain the goals for the event. Circulate attendance sheet. Review location of restrooms and fire/emergency exit details.

○ **Talking Points**

• We all have experienced getting caught up in the commercialization of the holidays.

• Parents/caregivers are often pressured to provide the "perfect" holiday experience for their children.

• This can translate into purchasing all the toys on children's wish lists.

• Worthwhile items foster socialization and increase learning.

• We will explore some of these items. Many are not expensive.

• Meanwhile, your children are experimenting with a variety of games and activities in the other room.

• At the end of the evening, parents/caregivers will rejoin their children to discover which games may be possible gift ideas for their children.

○ 10 minutes: **Read aloud** *The Gift of Nothing* by Patrick McDonnell. See Recommended Read-Alouds in Resource Packet for additional titles. Discuss:

• What was the best gift for Earl? (friendship, time spent together)

• What is the best gift you can give your child? (time spent together)

• What are "must-have" items on your children's wish lists? Will the items promote discussion and interaction with others? Will learning take place?

○ 15 minutes: **Board Games**

• **Talking Points**

▪ Ask: Have you considered giving your children board games? Does anyone enjoy a Family Game Night at their home? If so, please share details.

▪ A regularly scheduled Family Game Night is a great way to spend time with your children. Try it for a designated period of time and then evaluate how it's working. What are the benefits? What do you like best about it? What do the kids enjoy most?

▪ Set up the Connect Four board game or access it on the computer. Ask a volunteer to play with you.

- You can simply play a game with your child. This is **quality time**.
- Make it a better learning experience by "thinking aloud" about the strategies you use to determine the placement of game pieces. "Thinking aloud" means sharing your thoughts as you determine which action to take next or which action may cause you to lose the game and allows your child to gain insight. (Demonstrate as you and the volunteer play the game.)
- Ask: What skills are we modeling?
- Demonstrate how to be a gracious winner or loser. This is an important social skill.
- Practice "thinking aloud" as you play a game of Tic Tac Toe with the person sitting next to you.
- Find the Tic Tac Toe page of your handout.
- Play with a partner. Decide who will be X and O. Let's have X's go first.
- Before you make a mark, tell your partner how you decided placement.
- Continue playing, explaining your reasoning, until someone wins or a tie is declared.
- If someone forgets to "think aloud" before making a mark, the other person can ask, "Why did you put your mark there?"
- If time allows, play a second game, practicing the think aloud process.
- You can use the "think aloud" technique with almost any game you play with your child.
- The Resource Packet includes select websites that offer board and card games that can be played for free!

○ 10 minutes: **Building Sets and Craft Kits**

- **Talking Points**
  - In the Resource Packet you will find recommended sets and kits listed.
  - Purchasing large, expensive kits is not necessary. Kits can be found widely, including at discount and dollar stores.

- Be mindful of the age recommendations on the boxes. Purchasing a set or craft several years above your child's age might cause frustration. (Show example of age range listed on a toy box.)
- Working with your child can be precious bonding time, but be careful not to take over the project, even when your child experiences difficulty. Guide your child in problem-solving. Ask how the problem might be solved. Reread directions, study illustrations, undo a step, and try again.
- Set up a story context for building. For example, you might say, "This car is trying to get from the table to the chair but there is a river right here. What can we do? Can we build a bridge? Is the bridge wide enough for the car? Is it long enough to span the river? Would we have enough pieces to build the bridge if the river were wider?"
- Ask: What can your child learn from these kits? (creativity, planning, following directions, small motor development, satisfaction of completion of a project, problem-solving)
  ○ 10 minutes: **Other Gifts That Support Learning**
- **Talking Points**
  - Review the items on the list in the Resource Packet.
  - The websites listed are just a few examples of companies that carry educational toys. Check websites before purchasing to be sure they are legitimate.
  - Remind participants that books make great gifts. Book ownership is a proven predictor of literacy success. See Recommended Read-Alouds listed in the Resource Packet.
  - Give adults a bookplate for each child they brought to the event and suggest they use these when they purchase a book for the child. The child will know the book is a special gift.
  - Remind participants to spend time reading the book with the child. The best gift is the gift of time!
  ○ 10 minutes: **Closing the Literacy Booster Event**
  - Ask if there are any questions.
  - Ask participants to complete a brief evaluation of the event in order to offer valuable feedback for future events. (See Appendix for an example of an evaluation form.)
  - Request that parents/caregivers rejoin their child(ren) and ask them what they did and if they enjoyed the activities. Which was their favorite? Why?
  - Remind parents/caregivers that they can note their child's preferences on the wish list in the Resource Packet.
  - Thank all volunteers and participants for coming.

Bibliography

American Research Group, Inc., "2013 Christmas Gift Spending Plans Stall," accessed May 22, 2014, http://americanresearchgroup.com/holiday/

Bernier, Annie, Stephanie M. Carlson, and Natasha Whipple, "From External Regulation to Self-regulation: Early Parenting Precursors of Young Children's Executive Functioning," *Child Development* 81, no. 1 (January/February 2010): 326–339, doi: 10.1111/14678624200901387.x

Caldera, Yvonne M., Anne McDonald Culp, Marion O'Brien, Rosemarie T. Truglio, Mildred Alvarez, and Althea C. Huston, "Children's Play Preferences, Construction Play with Blocks, and Visual-spatial Skills: Are They Related?" *International Journal of Behavioral Development* 23, no. 4 (December 1999): 855–872, doi: 10.1080/016502599383577

Casey, Beth M., Nicole Andrews, Holly Schindler, Joanne E. Kersh, Alexandra Samper, and Juanita Copely, "The Development of Spatial Skills Through Interventions Involving Block Building Activities," *Cognition and Instruction* 26, no. 3 (2008): 269–309, doi: 10.1080/07370000802177177

Common Core State Standards, www.corestandards.org/Math/Practice/

Foster, Emily K. and Alycia M. Hund, "The Impact of Scaffolding and Overhearing on Young Children's Use of the Spatial Terms Between and Middle," *Journal of Child Language* 39, no. 2 (March 2012): 338–364, doi: 10.1017/S0305000911000158

Franklin, Sue, Mary Peat, and Alison Lewis, "Non-traditional Interventions to Stimulate Discussion: The Use of Games and Puzzles," *Journal of Biological Education* 37, no. 2 (2003): 79–84, doi: 10.1080/00219266.2003.9655856

Gobet, Fernand, Jean Retschitzki, and Alex de Voogt, *Moves in Mind: The Psychology of Board Games*. East Sussex, UK: Psychology Press, 2004.

MacVean, Mary, "For Many People, Gathering Possessions Is Just the Stuff of Life," *Los Angeles Times*, March 21, 2014, accessed December 9, 2014, http://articles.latimes.com/2014/mar/21/health/la-he-keeping-stuff-20140322

Reid, David, A., "Describing Reasoning in Early Elementary School Mathematics," *Teaching Children's Mathematics* (December 2002): 234–237.

Ramani, Geetha B. and Robert S. Siegler, "Promoting Broad and Stable Improvements in Low-Income Children's Numerical Knowledge Through Playing Number Board Games," *Child Development* 79, no. 2 (March/April 2008): 375–394, doi: 10.1111/14678624200701131

Sharp, Laura, A., "Stealth Learning: Unexpected Learning Opportunities Through Games," *Journal of Instructional Research* 1 (January 2012), accessed December 9, 2014, www.gcu.edu/Academics/Journal-of-Instructional-Research/-Unexpected-Learning-Opportunities-Through-Games-.php

Statista, "Average Amount Spent Per Child on Toys by Country in 2011," accessed May 22, 2014, www.statista.com/statistics/194424/amount-spent-on-toys-per-child-by-country-since-2009/

Resource Packet for Wrap It Up! can be found on the following pages. See also related Take-Home TipSheet in Chapter 12. TipSheets in color and in Spanish can be found in eResources online.

*Tired of trying to buy everything on your child's wish list?
Looking for gifts that support and may increase your
child's learning power?*

Bring the family and join us!
Wrap It Up!
Great Gifts for Great Kids

_____
Date and time

_____
Place

Please return registration form by

_____
Date

- -

Yes, I/we will attend the **Wrap It Up! Literacy Booster Event**

Parent(s)/Caregiver(s) _____

Teacher _____ Room _____

Number of adults attending _____

Number of children attending _____

Play is often talked about as if it were a relief from serious learning. But for children, play is serious learning.

—Mr. Rogers

Bookplates

This Book Belongs To

This Book Belongs To

This Book Belongs To

This Book Belongs To

This Book Belongs To

This Book Belongs To

Wrap It Up!
Parent/Caregiver Resource
Packet

Tic Tac Toe Game Boards

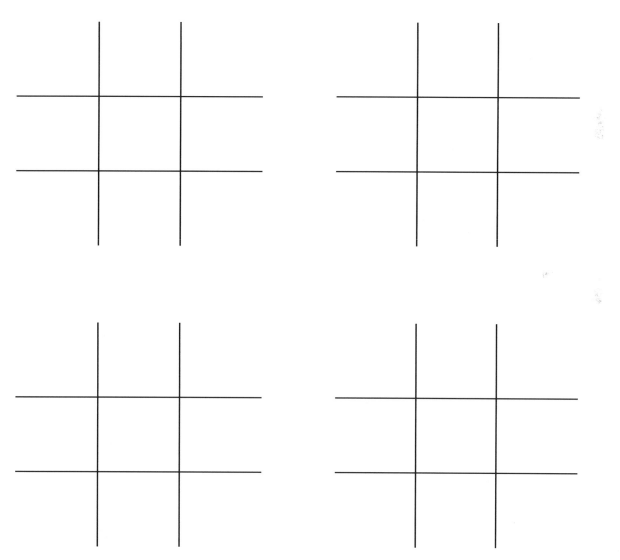

Board Games

Name of Game	Skills
Checkers	Strategy; planning
Chess	Strategy; planning; patience
Chutes and Ladders	Numbers, counting
Clue	Reasoning
Connect Four	Counting and other math concepts; planning; strategy
Dominoes	Counting; matching
Jenga	Fine motor skills
Make-Your-Own-opoly	Creativity; counting; money; strategy
Memory	Matching; visual memory
Mouse Trap	Cause/effect; chain reactions
Operation	Eye-hand coordination
Pictionary/ Pictionary, Jr.	Vocabulary; visual representation
Risk	Strategy
Scrabble/Scrabble, Jr.	Spelling; vocabulary
Scattergories	Vocabulary; similarities

Board Game Websites

www.pogo.com/board-games
www.pogo.com/misc/gamesearch/gamesearch.do?pageSec
tion=guest_home-game_search
www.mathisfun.com/games/connect4.html

Additional Games

Name of Game	Skills
Crossword puzzles	Vocabulary; spelling
Mazes	Eye-hand coordination; spatial relationships
Puzzles	Visual perception; planning; spatial relationships
Sudoku	Numerical relationships
Word search	Spelling; visual perception

Arts and Crafts

Kits

Models (car, plane, building, etc.)

Origami book and paper

Science lab kits

Stamp pads and stamps

Building Blocks

Best Lock	Lincoln Logs
Edushape EduBlocks	Mega Bloks
Erector	Nanoblocks
K'Nex	Wooden Blocks
Legos	

More Educational Gifts

Analog clock (numbers on a face rather than digital read-out)

Atlas

Books, Books, Books!

Calendar

Dictionary

Globe

Journal/Diary

Reading light

Thesaurus

Internet Shopping Sites

www.edutainment.com

www.aristoplay.com

www.hearthsong.com

www.themusicstand.com

www.spilsbury.com

www.learnandplay.com

www.constplay.com

www.youngexplorers.com

www.mindwareonline.com

My Child's Wish List

Recommended Read-Alouds

A Bus Called Heaven, by Bob Graham. Time spent giving new life to an abandoned bus unites an urban neighborhood in this feel-good modern fable. Ages 5–7.

The Day It Rained Hearts, by Felicia Bond. (Reissue of *Four Valentines in a Rainstorm*, 1983.) A young child determines the perfect gift for each of her friends. Ages 5–7.

Extra Yarn, by Mac Barnett, illustrated by Jon Klassen. Caldecott Honor. Annabelle uses a magical box of yarn to knit sweaters for her dog, classmates, Mr. Crabtree, and even a truck. Over time, changes occur in Annabelle's bleak town. When a greedy archduke steals the box, he's in for a big surprise. Delightful turn of events offers plenty of possibilities for discussion. Ages 5–8.

The Gift of Nothing, by Patrick McDonnell. From the Mutts comic strip creator; Mooch tries to discover the perfect gift for Earl. Ages 4–9.

Gifts of the Heart, by Patricia Polacco. After Gramma dies, Kay helps care for Richie and Trisha and teaches them about gifts that come from the heart. Ages 6–9.

Gracias Thanks, by Pat Mora, illustrated by John Parra. Bilingual text gently reminds readers of the many things we can express thanks for every day. Ages 4–7.

More Than Things: A Children's Book of Gifts, by Jen Burns, illustrated by Kati Burns. With a birthday coming soon, Brother's dream turns him from greedy to grateful. All ages.

Nothing, by Jon Agee. Modern fable about fads, shopping, and acquiring "stuff." All ages.

A Sick Day for Amos McGee, by Philip C. Stead, illustrated by Erin E. Stead. Caldecott Medal. Animals from the zoo visit their beloved friend Amos when he is too sick to come to work, offering him just what he needs to feel better. Ages 5–7.

Those Shoes, by Maribeth Boelts, illustrated by Noah Z. Jones. This realistic, heartwarming story based on the author's childhood experience focuses on needs versus wants and valuing friendship over fads. Ages 7–9.

Two Speckled Eggs, by Jennifer K. Mann. Ginger receives a birthday gift from Lyla, who is a little different from her peers, and a friendship begins. Ages 6–8.

CHAPTER 9

A Night Out with the Guys . . . and the Kids!
Encouraging Male Involvement in Literacy

Note: This session promotes positive interaction between the child and a male parent/ caregiver. This may include fathers, stepfathers, grandfathers, foster fathers, uncles, older brothers, or family friends who play an important role in the life of the child. Though the term "guys" is used in the materials, it should be noted that this event need not exclude female caregivers.

In the 21st century, the definition of "family" has evolved. In the United States, there no longer is a preponderance of two-parent homes in which one family member, usually Dad, works outside the home while Mom facilitates the running of the household, schedules the children's activities, and is responsible for managing homework and other school matters (McBride and Rane 1997). Blended families, one-parent households, two wage-earner families, other adults serving as guardians, and day care facilities offering after-school programs have increased in the last several decades. The effects of the changing home structure and challenging economic conditions have limited the amount of time families spend conversing, laughing, and reading together. What has not changed, however, is the effect that adults in the home can have on the literacy development of children. Parents/ caregivers benefit from understanding that learning can take place in a multitude of ways in the home.

Current research on the direct effects of children's interactions with fathers or other significant male role models is limited; however, findings that do exist clearly show that language and reading development of children is enhanced when parents/caregivers share activities, discuss events and experiences, and read with their children on a regular basis (McBride and Rane 1997; O'Brien and Shemilt 2003).

Fathers are becoming more involved in their children's education (Pleck 1997). Often, this is the result of a conscious decision to share responsibilities within the household, custody agreements, and work schedules. Some male caregivers are comfortable in this new role; others benefit from encouragement and increased awareness. An evening in which male caregivers are specifically invited to participate opens the door to increased adult/child interaction and learning. Children with male caregivers who are actively involved in their education show increased cognitive abilities (Yogman et al. 2005), are psychologically well-adjusted (Flouri 2005), and demonstrate increased social competence and healthier relationships with peers (Lamb 1997).

Photograph by Susan E. Busch. Used with permission.

Research suggests that male caregivers use varied and sometimes more challenging vocabulary than mothers (Lamb and Tamis-LeMonda 2003; Pancsofar and Vernon-Feagans 2006), and activities that encourage male caregivers' interactions with children may be beneficial. The Common Core State Standards require students to "participate effectively in a range of conversations . . . with diverse partners" (CCSS.ELA-Literacy.CCRA.SL.1) and "interpret words and phrases as they are used in a text . . ." (CCSS.ELA-Literacy. CCRA.R.4). Research indicates that male caregivers may be more reluctant to participate in print-related activities than mothers (Millard 1997). Other activities in which fathers can be engaged that may prove beneficial to children (Ortiz et al. 1999) include reading environmental print, newspapers, magazines, and manuals—and use of computers. Interactive play can also increase literacy development (Stockall and Dennis 2013). The activities in this session include a variety of literacy boosting practices.

A Night Out with the Guys . . . and the Kids!

Grade Levels: Pre-K–5

Time: 1.5 hours

Supplies
- Large room with tables and chairs to comfortably accommodate all participants
- Board games, card games, and letter dice
- Building blocks and plastic building sets
- Sports, hobby, and nature magazines
- Paper airplane materials
- Nonfiction books at appropriate reading levels
- Chart paper/whiteboard and markers
- Copies of game materials and instructions
- Read-aloud book
- Document reader, opaque projector, or another means for sharing the read-aloud book

Goals
- Male caregivers will participate in several activities that require them to read and converse with their child in an enjoyable, relaxed setting.
- Male caregivers will experience that any activity with children can be a learning opportunity.
- Male caregivers will help children read and accomplish engaging activities.
- Male caregivers will learn that they can help expand children's vocabulary through shared activities.

Family Literacy Event Planning

Several weeks in advance
- ❑ Select date, reserve room, and solicit assistance from faculty and staff.
- ❑ Collect and prepare materials.
- ❑ As event draws near, send home a special invitation to all "guys." Include a registration form to be returned to enable preparation of ample materials. (See example in Resource Packet.)

One week in advance
- ❑ Send reminder to families.
- ❑ Confirm arrangements and volunteers.
- ❑ Practice the read-aloud. You are modeling read-aloud behaviors you are hoping to foster in participants.

Day of the event

❑ Earlier in the day, set up the room. Place one or two activities on each table. Having sets of similar activities clustered on a table will allow more than one family at a time to enjoy the activity. With each activity, place instruction pages from Resource Packet that include:
  ○ directions for completing the activity,
  ○ the educational value of the activity,
  ○ and tips for positive interaction with children.
❑ As families arrive, greet them at the door and encourage them to browse the activities. Request that they not begin until directions have been given.

Leading the Family Literacy Event

○ 5 minutes: **Getting Started**

Begin promptly with a welcome, a brief introduction of all staff members present, a reminder to silence cell phones, and an overview of the goals for the event. Circulate attendance sheet. Review location of restrooms and fire/emergency exit details.

○ **Talking Points**
  • You are here to have fun!
  • Learning takes place during many kinds of activities at home. Talking about the activities with your child opens communication and expands vocabulary.
  • You will be enjoying several activities tonight. Some materials may be taken home, such as the paper airplanes. Others, such as the Legos, must remain here. Please follow the instructions on the tables.
  • Converse while you work together. Talking with your child increases vocabulary, which impacts learning.

○ 10 minutes: **Read-aloud**

Begin with a read-aloud such as *My Dad, My Hero*, by Ethan Long, or *Dad's Dinosaur Day*, by Diane Dawson Hearn. (See Recommended Read-Aloud list in Resource Packet for additional suggestions.)

○ 15 minutes: **Directions for Participants**

○ **Talking Points**
  • You and your child may choose an activity together. (Briefly explain the activities at each table.)
  • Sit beside one another, read the instructions, and complete the activity.
  • Talk about what you are doing, what choices you are making as you play or create, and why you are making those choices.
  • When experiencing difficulty with an activity, discuss options, such as starting over, re-reading the directions, or asking for help.
  • If you complete an activity, feel free to move to another.
  • Questions?

- 20 minutes: **First Activity**
  - Parents/caregivers and children choose an activity.
  - Leaders circulate, assist with directions, and encourage discussion among parents/caregivers and children, and with others at the table.
- 20 minutes: **Second Activity**
  - After 20 minutes, families move to second activity.
- 15 minutes: **Wrap-Up**
  - Request that families work to complete the current activity.
  - Lead a brief discussion about the learning that took place. Take brief notes on chart paper/whiteboard. Consider publishing notes in a follow-up communication. Ask:
    - Which activities did you enjoy the most and why?
    - What did you learn about your child at this event?
    - What new words did your child learn?
    - Would you consider incorporating such activities into your weekly routines at home? Discuss.
- 5 minutes: **Closing the Family Literacy Event**
  - Ask participants to complete a brief evaluation of this event in order to offer valuable feedback for future events. (See Appendix for an example of an evaluation form.)
  - Thank volunteers and participants for coming.
  - Parents/caregivers may wish to talk with facilitator privately rather than in an open forum. Be approachable but keep it brief. Smile!

Suggested Activities

Board Games
Commercial board games usually take longer to complete than the allotted time. Simple games can be drawn on poster board or generated from the computer. Game tokens can be coins, erasers, or tokens from board games. Cards with directions for advancing on the board can be created on the computer. (See sample in eResources online.)

Letter Dice Games
Many classrooms have letter dice. Players place 5–6 dice in a plastic cup. Taking turns, they shake the dice, and spill them onto the table. In 2 minutes, players try to make as many words as they can from the letters. An egg timer is recommended. Paper should be provided for keeping score. (See sample in eResources online.)

Magazines
Select several magazines that will appeal to a variety of interests, such as *Sports Illustrated for Kids, Highlights, Ranger Rick, National Geographic Kids, Yum Food, Fun for Kids*, and *Boys' Life*. Place pencils and 3 × 5 cards on the table for participants to note interesting facts or statistics they read.

Small Building Sets

Photograph by Kathryn Walker. Used with permission.

Purchase small packages of building sets, such as Legos or Mega Bloks, in which specific directions need to be followed to create the form. Place pieces and directions in slide-closure plastic bags. Make sure table instructions remind participants to dismantle the form after they have completed it so that another family may enjoy the activity.

Nonfiction or Informational Books
Display a variety of nonfiction or informational books on various topics. Include pencils and small notebooks, which could be as simple as blank paper stapled into booklets. Directions request that parents and students draw pictures, note interesting details they learn, or write down questions or topics for future research.

Wooden or Plastic Building Blocks
Place assorted blocks (cubes, cylinders, cones) on the table. Using Task Cards (see Resource Packet), participants build according to directions. Vary difficulty.

Pre-printed Paper Airplanes
Provide plenty of colorful paper and folding instructions so students can take them home. Designate a target or landing area to prevent airplanes from flying toward participants. Web-sites offer a variety of paper airplane plans, from easy to difficult:
www.amazingpaperairplanes.com/Simple.html
www.ncgraphicarts.com/ryan/other/planes.htm
www.origami-instructions.com/paper-airplanes.html
www.scribd.com/collections/3107807/Civil-Air-Patrol-Paper-Airplanes
Printing directions on color-coded paper according to difficulty is recommended; for example, green for easy, yellow for moderate difficulty, and red for most difficult.

Modifications for Pre-K and Kindergarten Students

An activity night with a male caregiver is especially important for younger children. It may set the pattern for continuing interaction, conversation, and learning together throughout childhood. A Night Out with the Guys event can be modified in the following ways:

- With shorter attention spans, children in preschool or kindergarten need activities that can be completed in less time. Allow 8–10 minutes per activity.
- Lengthy written directions can be simplified or illustrated with pictures.
- Young children are tactile and require movement; prepare activities that allow participants to be active.

Board Games
Create simple board games using colored dots in random sequence. A deck of cards, each with a colored dot, requires players to advance to the spot of that color. Game boards using pictures of animals or foods would involve discussion of the characteristics of the pictured object.

Magazines
Suggested magazines for the younger set include *Turtle* magazine for preschool kids, *Your Big Backyard*, National Wildlife Federation's *Wild Animal Baby, National Geographic Little Kids*, and Highlights' *High Five*.

Nonfiction or Informational Books
Display nonfiction texts in a variety of subject areas. Provide paper and crayons or colored pencils so children and caregivers can illustrate what they learn.

Dress Up
On one table place items of clothing that require participants to tie, zip, snap, Velcro, button, or fold. Provide a checklist on which to designate what the child can do independently or with help.

Exercise Time
Designate an area with rugs or mats where the caregiver and child can perform sit-ups, toe touches, squats, arm circles (forward and backward), jumping jacks, broad jumps, and various stretches. Post pictures, arrows, and a few words to demonstrate the tasks. Count to 10 for each exercise.

Bibliography

Common Core State Standards, accessed June 2, 2013, www.corestandards.org/ELA-Literacy/, 10, 22.

Flouri, Eirini, *Fathering and Child Outcomes*. London: Wiley, 2005.

Lamb, Michael E., ed., *The Role of the Father in Child Development*, 3rd ed. Hoboken, NJ: Wiley, 1997.

Lamb, Michael E. and Catherine S. Tamis-LeMonda, "The Role of the Father: An Introduction" in *The Role of the Father in Child Development*, 4th ed., ed. Michael E. Lamb, 1–31, Hoboken, NJ: Wiley, 2003.

McBride, Brent A. and Thomas R. Rane, "Role Identity, Role Investments, and Paternal Involvement: Implications for Parenting Programs for Men," *Early Childhood Research Quarterly* 12, no. 2 (1997): 173–197, doi:10.1016/S0885-2006(97)90013-2

Millard, Elaine, "Differently Literate: Gender Identity and Construction of the Developing Reader," *Gender and Education* 9, no. 1 (1997): 31–49, doi:10.1080/09540259721439

O'Brien, Margaret and Ian Shemilt, *Working Fathers: Earning and Caring*. Great Britain: Equal Opportunities Commission, 2003.

Ortiz, Robert, Stephen Stile, and Christopher Brown, "Early Literacy Activities of Fathers: Reading and Writing with Young Children," *Young Children* 54, no. 5 (September 1999): 16–18.

Pancsofar, Nadya and Lynne Vernon-Feagans, "Mother and Father Language Input to Young Children: Contributions to Later Language Development," *Journal of Applied Developmental Psychology* 27, no. 6 (November–December 2006): 571–587, doi:10.1016/j.appdev.2006.08.003

Pleck, Joseph R., "Parental Involvement: Levels, Sources, and Consequences," in *The Role of the Father in Child Development*, 3rd ed., ed. Michael E. Lamb, 66–103, New York: Wiley, 1997.

Stockall, Nancy and Lindsay Dennis, "Fathers' Role in Play: Enhancing Early Language and Literacy of Children with Developmental Delays," *Early Childhood Education Journal* 41, no. 4, (July 2013): 299–306, doi:10.1007/s10643-012-0557-2

Yogman, Michael W., Daniel Kindlon, and Felton Earls, "Father Involvement and Cognitive/Behavioral Outcomes of Preterm Infants," *Journal of the American Academy of Child and Adolescent Psychiatry* 34, no. 1 (January 2005): 58–66, doi:10.1097/00004583-199501000-00015

Resource Packet for A Night Out with the Guys . . . and the Kids! can be found on the following pages. See also related Take-Home TipSheet in Chapter 12. TipSheets in color and in Spanish can be found in eResources online.

A Night Out with the Guys . . .
and the Kids!

Hey Big Guy,

You are invited to a special evening of literacy activities with your child.

Games   **Fun**   **Magazines**
            Learning   **Books**

Join us on:

Time:

Place:

Please fill out registration form and return by _____

We will attend **A Night Out with the Guys!**

Name _____

Teacher _____

Contact info _____ Number attending _____

A Night Out with the Guys . . . and the Kids!
Parent/Caregiver Resource Packet

Game Instructions

1. Choose a game token.
2. Shuffle the cards and place them face down.
3. Take turns choosing a card and completing the activity.
4. If you complete the activity successfully, move ahead.
5. If you do not complete the activity, you must go back 1 space.
6. First person to the finish line wins!

Learning

Reading, following directions, taking turns, counting, and winning or losing politely

Tips

Do not let your child win. Guys should model winning or losing graciously.

If your child cannot complete the activity, talk about why. Do not give answers.

Give encouragement at all times. When child completes a difficult task, praise the effort.

Game Card Deck 1

Name 5 fruits. Move ahead 3 spaces.	Name 3 cities. Move ahead 2 spaces.	Name 2 states. Forward 3 spaces.
What is a noun? Move ahead 3 spaces.	What is a verb? Move ahead 4 spaces.	Give an example of a synonym. Move ahead 3 spaces.
How are a cat and a lion alike? Advance 3 spaces.	What is the opposite of dark? Forward 1 space.	What do plants need to grow? Advance 3 spaces.
Name 5 farm animals. Move ahead 2 spaces.	Name 2 oceans. Move ahead 3 spaces.	Name 3 books by Dr. Seuss. Move ahead 4 spaces.
Name 3 vehicles. Move ahead 1 space.	Name 4 ocean creatures. Move ahead 2 spaces.	Name 5 shapes. Move ahead 4 spaces.

Being a role model is the most powerful form of educating.

—John Wooden

Game Card Deck 2

Do 8 jumping jacks. Move ahead 1 space.	Touch your toes 10 times. Move ahead 2 spaces.	Moon walk 8 steps. Move ahead 3 spaces.
Pretend to row a boat. Move ahead 1 space.	Count by 5's to 50. Move ahead 3 spaces.	Sing a song. Move ahead 4 spaces.
Pretend to climb stairs. Move ahead 1 space.	Do 10 arm circles. Move ahead 2 spaces.	Do 6 sit-ups. Move ahead 3 spaces.
March around the table. Move ahead 2 spaces.	Pretend to play a flute. Move ahead 1 space.	Turn around 3 times. Move ahead 2 spaces.
Jump like a frog. Move ahead 2 spaces.	Hop 7 times on 1 foot. Move ahead 1 space.	Make 3 animals noises. Move ahead 3 spaces.

Letter Dice Instructions

1. One person shakes the dice in the cup.

2. Carefully spill the dice onto the table.

3. Start the timer.

4. In 3 minutes, see how many real words you can make from the letters on the dice.

5. Write the words down on the score card. Have the other person check the spelling.

6. You may reuse the letters in new words.

7. Now the other person takes a turn.

Source: Shutterstock.

Learning

Manipulating letters to form words

Taking turns

Writing and spelling words correctly

Tips

Encourage children to think about rhyming patterns.

When correcting spelling, encourage children to look for the error.

If children become frustrated, give hints but do not tell them how to make a new word.

Magazine Reading

1. Choose one to read together.

2. Have 3 x 5 cards handy.

3. Read to your child, have your child read to you, or take turns.

4. After a page or two, talk about what you have learned.

5. Write what you have learned on the cards.

Learning

When your child sees you reading, it becomes more valuable.

Talking about what you have learned or sharing experiences you have had helps your child relate to what they are reading on a more personal level.

Your child is expanding his/her vocabulary.

Tips

Just enjoy the time together. Don't worry about fast or "perfect" reading.

Don't ask your child to "sound out" the word when you are reading for enjoyment. Tell your child the word and keep going.

Building Blocks Instructions

1. Shuffle the task cards.

2. Choose a card.

3. Read the task carefully.

4. Discuss different ways to complete the task.

5. Choose a plan and work together.

Learning

How to follow steps in a process

How to use diagrams to assist with understanding directions

How to handle frustration and work to solve a problem

Tips

Enjoy the experience with your child.

Do not build it for your child; work as a team.

Offer suggestions and guidance.

Help your child experience success.

Building Blocks Task Cards

Build a tower using as many blocks as you can.	Build a house with a chimney.
Construct a bridge.	Build a castle.
Construct a building with double towers.	Construct a pyramid.
Make a vehicle.	Make the longest building possible.

My father gave me the greatest gift anyone could give another person: he believed in me.

—Jim Valvano

Small Building Sets Instructions

1. Unzip the bag and carefully take out all the pieces and directions.
2. Read or look at all the directions first.
3. Follow the directions in order.
4. When you have completed building, take it apart and place all pieces back in the bag.

Learning

Following steps in a process

Using diagrams to assist with understanding directions

Handling frustration and working to solve a problem

Tips

Enjoy the experience with your child.

Do not build it for your child; work as a team.

Offer suggestions and guidance.

Help your child experience success.

The thrill of being a great father is not seeing your children go on to become successful adults. The thrill of a great father is the journey, experiencing your child's successes along the pathway to their greatness.

—Reed Markham

Informational Book Reading

1. Choose a notebook and write your names on the cover.

2. Pick a book together. Read to your child, have your child read to you, or take turns reading.

3. After a page or two, talk about what you've learned.

Source: Shutterstock.

4. Use the notebook to write about what you have learned, or a related experience you have had.

Learning

When your child sees you reading, it becomes more valuable.

Talking about what you have learned, or sharing experiences you have had allows children to relate to what they are reading on a more personal level.

Your child is expanding his/her vocabulary.

Tips

Just enjoy the time together.

Don't worry about fast or "perfect" reading.

Help your child if he is stuck. Don't stop to have him "sound out" words. Give a hint or tell him the word.

Recommended Read-Alouds

Daddies Do It Different, by Alan Lawrence Sitomer, illustrated by Abby Carter. Dad undertakes everyday tasks, leading to laughter and fun. Ages 4–8.

Dad's Dinosaur Day, by Diane Dawson Hearn. When Dad wakes up and isn't acting himself, Mom says he's having a Dinosaur Day. Mikey and Dad have fun all day, but Mikey wants his old dad back. Ages 4–8.

Flying Machines, by Nick Arnold, illustrated by Brendan Kearney. An interactive book that teaches aerodynamics and includes five models to construct. Talk about fun and learning! Ages 8 and up.

Guess How Much I Love You?, by Sam McBratney, illustrated by Anita Jeram. Nutbrown Hare and Father try to outdo one another demonstrating their love. Ages 2–5.

Mighty Dads, by Joan Holub, illustrated by James Dean. Construction site dads teach their little ones to do their best! Ages 4–6.

My Dad Is a Superhero, by Lily Lexington. A boy explains all his dad's superpowers, but even if Dad had no power, they'd still love each other. Ages 4–8.

My Dad Is Big and Strong, BUT, by Coralie Saudo, illustrated by Kris Di Giacomo. A child experiences the difficulties of putting Dad to bed and gains insight into his own bedtime routine. Ages 3–8.

My Dad, My Hero, by Ethan Long. A dad may not have super powers, but he is still a hero to his child. Ages 4–8.

My Dad the Pirate, by David Durbin. A young boy uses his imagination to demonstrate the things his dad does as a pirate . . . and he's the first mate. Ages 5–8.

Tickle Monster, by Josie Bissett, illustrated by Kevan Atteberry. An alien comes to Earth to bring laughter through tickling. Promotes family interaction. Ages 2–7.

Tyrannosaurus Dad, by Liz Rosenberg, illustrated by Matthew Myers. A young boy sees his dad as a Tyrannosaurus who is too busy to pay attention. Dad shows he does care when he comes to his son's aid at a baseball game. Ages 4–8.

What Daddies Do Best, by Laura Joffe Numeroff, illustrated by Lynn Munsinger. Things daddies can do to show their love. Ages 4–8.

CHAPTER 10

Celebrating Us!
Our Culture and Heritage
Sharing Stories, Food, Traditions, and Goodwill

The United States of America: A Melting Pot

The use of the phrase "melting pot" began in the early 1900s to convey the idea that, as mostly white Anglo-Saxon European immigrants came to the United States, they very much desired to become "Americanized." Immigrants typically settled in ethnic neighborhoods where they felt more comfortable and accepted as they assimilated into the American culture. Immigrants strived to speak American English and dress like Americans (Gordon 1964). That was the norm: Their public persona was to look, sound, and *be* American, although among close family and friends, immigrants often continued to practice European traditions and customs.

The Immigration Act of 1990 dramatically raised the number of immigrants entering the United States. The nation has become more like a trail mix than a melting pot. Groups emigrating from Asia, Africa, and South America—some who come willingly, and some who feel compelled to leave their homes because of unrest in their country—are more able to keep their ethnic culture vibrant because of their large numbers (Alba and Nee 1997). Technology allows immigrants to keep in touch with family and friends abroad (McDonald and Balgopal 1998). Immigrant families often share their culture with others and speak of their heritage proudly. They celebrate traditions at neighborhood or school cultural fairs, church festivals, and other festivities. Immigrants may not speak English or may prefer to proudly wear customary native dress. They may own stores that sell food and other items imported from their country of origin, much like the European immigrants of a generation before. Like their predecessors, twenty-first century immigrants may choose to live in ethnic neighborhoods, but their neighborhoods may be comprised of immigrants from various regions of the world. In the United States, people from a variety of cultures live and work together, but in some ways, like trail mix, they remain distinct in their "flavors." Celebrating diverse cultures brings understanding, acceptance, and inclusion. Literature helps children learn about the peoples of the world and encourages acceptance of differences (Gay 2000).

When there is open and positive inclusion of all cultures, students from other nations learn more readily and develop a sense of belonging to the larger school group (Berry 1997).

The Common Core Learning Standards require students to determine the meanings of words and phrases in a text. By reading quality multicultural literature with students, educators expose children to varied vocabulary. We can lead discussions regarding the meaning and use of specific words to increase vocabulary development (Brand and Harper 2010). One Common Core standard (CCSS.ELA-Literacy.CCRA.R.6) suggests that students assess how point of view influences content and style of text. Learning about the cultural and ideological views of people around the world broadens students' understanding, appreciation, and acceptance of differing points of view.

A school-wide multicultural event may take many forms. Sharing cultures through the use of literature has its roots in oral storytelling. Over hundreds of years, families have passed down rich traditions and core beliefs through story. The quality and availability of multicultural literature has increased greatly over the past few decades. Both educational and trade publishers feature multicultural literature in their collections. Online resources for fiction and informational books, such as Asia for Kids, Culture for Kids, Mantralingua, and Language Lizard, join multicultural children's publishers such as Lee & Low. In addition to books, other educational resources, such as posters, games, toys, and flash cards are available to extend knowledge. School and public librarians possess a wealth of information on multicultural resources, can access resources readily, and are eager to assist. To broaden exposure to a variety of cultures, have each classroom choose a country other than those targeted for the Family Literacy Event. Students can research information to design posters, flags, and information boards about the country. Read multicultural literature pertinent to the nation or examine the immigrant experience through a child's eyes. See the Recommended Read-Aloud list in the Teacher Resources and additional suggestions in eResources online.

An optional feature of the Celebrate Us! Family Literacy Event is the Tasting Station. This portion of the event requires detailed planning and organization, but it is well worth the effort. Families are eager to share traditional or favorite foods, and students are more likely to be adventurous and try unfamiliar foods when presented with a variety of dishes their peers enjoy at home.

If recent immigrants are part of the school population, enlist the support and participation of ESOL/ELL teachers. Support personnel are valuable liaisons who can encourage families with whom they work to participate in school events. It helps immigrant students to know that their culture is respected and that they have something worthwhile to offer their peers. They can help build knowledge of and respect for cultural differences.

Higher learning institutions can serve as additional resources for multicultural events. Pre-service education students may volunteer to assist with crafts at culture stations, to help as greeters, or to assist as Tasting Station servers or Celebration Passport documenters. Many colleges and universities have cultural clubs that can provide ethnic dress, literature, musicians, or ethnic dancers. Such activities add to the experience or may be planned in place of the Tasting Station. By working as a community, we help students develop a wider view of the many cultures represented in our country.

Title: Celebrating Us! Our Culture and Heritage

Grade Levels: Grades K–5

Time: 2.5–3 hours

Supplies
- Auditorium or other large gathering place
- Six to eight classrooms to be used as Culture Stations, or gymnasium equipped with dividers
- A volunteer to staff each station
- Large sign to designate each Culture Station
- Multicultural children's books to display
- Read-aloud books for Culture Stations
- Document reader, opaque projector, or another means for sharing the whole group read-aloud book for opening the event (optional)
- Craft materials and instructions (placed in plastic bags) for each Culture Station
- Celebration Passports for all participant families (See Teacher Resources.)
- Rubber stamps and stamp pads

Tasting Station (optional)
- Cafeteria or large meeting room
- Tables and chairs to seat all comfortably
- Ample volunteers to help serve food
- Electrical outlets available for roasters or crock pots
- Extension cords
- Plastic tablecloths for serving tables
- 8″–9″ plates
- Cutlery
- Napkins
- Juice
- Cups
- Trash and recycling containers
- Cleaning supplies

Goals

- Families will listen to read-alouds and enjoy stories from different cultures.
- Families will learn about various cultures.
- Families will complete crafts representative of several cultures.
- Families will sample ethnic foods from a variety of cultures.
- Families may share personal experiences specific to their culture as well as experiences with cultures other than their own.

Literacy Booster Event Planning

Several months in advance

- ❑ Select date, reserve rooms, and solicit assistance from faculty, staff, and parent organization.
- ❑ Decide on the length of the event. A story and simple craft can be completed within a 20–30 minute session; however, facilitators may wish to adjust the time to suit the needs of the school population. The craft may be started in the Culture Station and completed at home, if necessary.
- ❑ Alert custodial staff to needs for the event.
- ❑ Begin advertising the event: posters, local newspaper article, district and school newsletters, parent organization communications, and classroom notices.
- ❑ Choose six to eight countries to feature at the Culture Stations. Enlist the aid of parents/caregivers or search websites for crafts representative of each country. (See Craft and Multicultural Book Sources.) Crafts may range from simple paper construction and coloring to wooden or clay crafts. (See samples in the Teacher Resources.) Budget and time constraints will determine choices. Create simple instruction pages and make copies.
- ❑ Select multicultural picture books from libraries, teacher collections, or colleges, or purchase from bookstores. (See Recommended Read-Alouds in the Teacher Resources and in eResources online.)
- ❑ Solicit a person to be in charge of the Tasting Station. (See Tasting Station checklist.)

Six weeks in advance

- ❑ Send invitations to all families. Ask for volunteers to make simple ethnic foods representative of their heritage or culture. (See sample in Teacher Resources.)

A few weeks in advance

- ❑ Ask classroom teachers to select a country from a list that includes the six to eight targeted cultures. (See suggestions in eResources online.)
  - ○ Classrooms can construct large flags to post outside their doors to designate the featured countries.

- Students can research the word for "hello" or "welcome" in that country and post it on the classroom door.
- If time allows, students in each classroom could research interesting information about the country and design posters to place alongside the flag.

❑ Send home an informational flyer with registration form to enable preparation of the rooms and ensure ample materials. (See Teacher Resources.)

❑ Prepare Celebration Passports. (See Teacher Resources.) Make double-sided copies and fold vertically. Choose passport stamps and stamp pads to represent each Culture Station.

❑ Alert custodial staff to the schedule for the event, including set-up and clean-up times.

❑ Purchase or prepare materials for crafts. Place materials and simple instructions in individual re-sealable bags. This will enable participants to take materials home if craft is not completed during the session.

❑ Assign volunteers to classrooms.

❑ Prepare Culture Station volunteers by providing the book, story summary, possible discussion points, craft sample, and directions in advance of event.

The day of the event

❑ Post signage at each Culture Station.

❑ Place stamp and stamp pad at entrance to each room.

❑ Make sure there is a large area cleared for students to sit on the floor and enough chairs for parents/caregivers to sit near students at each Culture Station.

❑ All craft materials should be set up and ready to use.

Leading the Literacy Booster Event

o 20 minutes: Start promptly in the auditorium. As students arrive, distribute Celebration Passports. (See Teacher Resources.) Begin with a warm welcome, a brief introduction of all staff present, a reminder to silence all cell phones, and an explanation of the goals of the event. Circulate attendance sheet. Review the location of restrooms and fire/emergency exit details.

o **Talking points**
- We are proud of our multicultural heritage. We come from varied backgrounds and have much to learn from one another. Tonight we will be participating in a variety of events, from enjoying read-alouds and constructing crafts to tasting ethnic foods—all of which celebrate various cultures.
- Read aloud *Goal!* by Sean Taylor, illustrated by Caio Vilela. Lead a brief discussion focusing on the fact that soccer, or fútbol, is enjoyed by people around the world. What other activities do we have in common? (Optional. See other Recommended Read-Alouds.)

- Explain that there are six/eight Culture Stations. (Refer to the Celebration Passport.) At each station, participants will hear a story and have a chance to work on a simple craft.
- Participants choose to visit four of the six/eight Culture Stations.
- Give participants an opportunity to read over the information about various stations and select those that may be of interest. Note that the room numbers are listed on the Celebration Passport and signs are posted on the doors.
- Participants will have 20–30 minutes to spend at each Culture Station. An announcement to move to the next station will be made over the public address system.
- The Tasting Station will be the final activity. After attending four sessions (Culture Stations), participants will join others at the Tasting Station to sample foods from different countries. (If there will not be a Tasting Station, the Culture Station sessions could be lengthened.)

o Participants proceed to the stations of their choice.

o Monitor the Tasting Station. Circulate and talk with participants about what they experienced. Encourage families to talk with one another about their experiences.

o At the end of the event, thank volunteers. Thank participants for attending. Remind parents/caregivers to take home pots, pans, bowls, and utensils they brought with them.

o Begin cleanup when most families are dispersing. Often, parents/caregivers or students will help when they see others cleaning up. This develops a sense of responsibility and community as well as camaraderie.

Teacher Resources for Celebrating Us! Our Culture and Heritage can be found on the following pages. See also related Take-Home TipSheet in Chapter 12. TipSheets in color and in Spanish can be found in eResources online.

Celebrating Us!
Teacher Resources
Our Culture and
Heritage

Colleagues,

    We will be holding a Multicultural Celebration on

_____

from

_____

There will be six to eight Culture Stations comprising a read-aloud and a simple craft or activity. We have selected books to read aloud and discuss; and the craft or activity materials and directions will be supplied, but we need volunteers to staff stations!

Culture Station activities will last about 20 minutes and will be repeated four times throughout the event.
Can you help?

Please contact _____

By _____

Thanks so much! This will be a fun time!

Celebrating Us! Our Culture and Heritage

Join us for a fun-filled event!

Date:

Time:

Place:

Stories! Fun! Food! Crafts!

Tasting Station Checklist

Six weeks in advance

- ☐ Send flyers home to request donations of ethnic foods.
- ☐ Determine time for set up and food drop off (most people will bring food when they come for the event).
- ☐ Enlist volunteers to help serve food, set up, and clean up.
- ☐ Connect with ESOL/ELL teachers and enlist help encouraging families to donate food and attend the event.
- ☐ Request use of school refrigerator for the day of the event.

Photograph by Susan E. Busch.

Four weeks in advance

- ☐ Maintain a list of volunteers, phone numbers, and foods.
- ☐ Check for electrical outlets and/or extension cords.
- ☐ Make a diagram of the placement of tables for plates, food, and drinks.
- ☐ Arrange to use school cutlery and dishes. If this is not feasible, purchase or solicit donations of plastic tablecloths, coated plates, cups, forks, napkins, and serving tools.

One week in advance

- ☐ Contact volunteers providing food and confirm set-up/drop-off times.
- ☐ Confirm volunteers assisting at Culture Stations.
- ☐ Gather food prep supplies, serving tools, and cleaning supplies.

The day of event

- ☐ Set up serving tables and strategically place trash receptacles.
- ☐ Place food in refrigerator, if needed.
- ☐ Arrange room temperature food on tables.
- ☐ Plug in roasters and crock pots; set at required temperature.
- ☐ Assign volunteers to check food temperature periodically prior to serving.
- ☐ 15 minutes before Tasting Station opens, place refrigerated food on tables.
- ☐ Pour juice into glasses/cups.
- ☐ Servers take their places at assigned stations (many foods can be self-serve but may be hot and require assistance for safety reasons). Foods should be portioned by volunteer servers.
- ☐ Clean up: Volunteers wipe down tables and align chairs, sweep floors, and collect trash and recyclables.

Celebrating Us!
Our Culture and
Heritage

We are hosting a Multicultural Event on

_____

We are planning a Tasting Station at which families will be invited to sample foods from other countries and cultures. If you are willing to prepare a cultural dish, please fill out the form below. Please note:

- Prepare sample sizes rather than full-sized portions.

- If food needs to remain hot, please bring a roaster or crock pot. Electrical outlets are available.

- Finger foods are preferred, but utensils will be available. (No soups, please.)

- Please print the name of the food, a simple description of the dish, and a list of ingredients on a 5 x 8 card.

Return form below by _____

- -

I/We will be happy to provide an ethnic dish for the **Celebrating Us! Multicultural Event**

Name _____

Phone Number _____

Name of Food _____

Please indicate: The dish needs to be kept cold before serving.   Yes   No

I will bring a roaster/crock pot and will need use of an outlet.   Yes   No

Celebrating Us!
Our Culture and Heritage

Multicultural Family Literacy Event

_____

Date and time

_____

Place

Stories!   Activities!   Crafts!   Food!   Fun!

Come Join Us!

Please register by _____

I/We will attend the **Celebrating Us! Multicultural Event** on

_____

Name _____

Phone number _____

Number attending: adults _____   students _____

Culture Stations

ℰℂℛℬ

Room _____ Culture_____

Book _____

Room _____ Culture_____

Book _____

Room _____ Culture_____

Book _____

Room _____ Culture_____

Book _____

Room _____ Culture_____

Book _____

Room _____ Culture_____

Book _____

Room _____ Culture_____

Book _____

Room _____ Culture_____

Book _____

Tasting Room

Foods I Liked: Country

_____   _____

_____   _____

_____   _____

_____   _____

_____   _____

ℰℂℛℬ

Celebration Passport of

_____

Celebrating Us!
Our Culture and Heritage

School

Date

Place

stamp	_____ country

_____
book title

Notes: _____

_____

_____

stamp	_____ country

_____
book title

Notes: _____

_____

_____

stamp	_____ country

_____
book title

Notes: _____

_____

_____

stamp	_____ country

_____
book title

Notes: _____

_____

_____

Thank you for volunteering to help at a
Culture Station at our

Celebrating Us! Multicultural Event

Your craft station will be _____

in Room _____. Materials and directions will be provided.

Please plan to arrive by _____.

You will be reading aloud _____.

It reflects the people and culture of _____.

Book summary:

Please prepare by reading the book prior to the event. Use expression while reading and hold the book so all can view the pictures. Enjoy reading aloud to your groups!

Possible discussion questions:

Before reading:
- Show the cover. Ask: What do you know about this nation and its people?
- Is this book about modern life or long ago? How do you know?

After reading, ask:
- What new ideas did you learn from this book?
- What do the illustrations show us about this country?
- What new or unfamiliar words did you notice? What do you think they mean?

If you have questions, please contact: _____

Craft Ideas for Culture Stations

Crafts should be able to be completed within 10–15 minutes. Place craft materials in re-sealable plastic bags. This will allow families to take materials home if they are unable to complete the craft during the session. Ideas for simple cultural crafts follow. Other ideas can be found in eResources online. For additional directions and examples, search "Country name crafts for kids" or check websites, such as Pinterest.

Central American Rain Stick: The rain stick is believed to have been invented by the Aztecs. It was used to help bring on rain. Use small diameter wrapping paper tubes, small screws or nails, wood colored contact paper and small beads or rice to make an entertaining rain stick.

Photograph by Mark Andrew Busch.

East Indian Thumbprint Peacock: The peacock is the national bird of India. Draw the bird's body and head on white copy paper and draw straight lines out from the body and add fine lines to look like fringe.

Photograph by Mark Andrew Busch.

Assemble blue, purple, green, and/or turquoise stamp pads. Have students use their thumbs and fingers to make oval shapes for peacock feathers. (Pattern can be found in eResources online.)

Eskimo Inuksuk Rock Craft: An Inuksuk was a large rock shape used by natives in northern North America to designate important areas. You will need cardboard squares, various shaped flat stones, and craft glue or a glue gun. Have students arrange stones in the Inuksuk (person) shape and glue into place. A glue gun works best and dries quickly but requires close supervision.

Photograph by Mark Andrew Busch.

Kenyan Sunset Watercolor: The African grasslands produce beautiful sunsets. In advance, prepare elephant, giraffe, rhino, ostrich, monkey, lion, and tiger shapes cut from black paper. Students can use red/orange/yellow or blue/yellow/purple water color paint to make a layered color design on paper. Glue animal shapes onto painted background to look like silhouettes against the setting sun. Alternative: Animal patterns can be traced and colored in with black marker or crayon.

Photograph by Mark Andrew Busch.

Native American Dream Catcher: Some Native American tribes believe that dream catchers protect children from nightmares. You will need a cardboard hoop with 8–10 notches cut into its sides, feathers, and colorful yarn. Show students how to wind yarn on the hoop to make a spider web design. Tie a piece of yarn to the top and attach one to three feathers onto this string. Add beads to the yarn on the top or bottom (optional).

Pakistani Henna Hands: The Pakistani people use henna to create complicated designs on their skin. Students can trace a handprint onto white paper and decorate with various designs using black marker.

Photograph by Mark Andrew Busch.

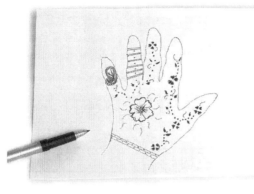

Photograph by Mark Andrew Busch.

Philippine Paról (star): Paróls are traditional ornamental Christmas stars. Five-pointed stars are cut from sturdy cardstock. Holes are punched into the top point and the bottom two points. Tie a string to the top to act as a hanger. Tie several pieces of colorful ribbon to the bottom points and cut to look like fringe. A simple shape can be drawn on the middle of the star.

Photograph by Mark Andrew Busch.

Russian Paper Matryoshka Dolls: The nested matryoshka dolls were first carved in Russia in the late 1800s. Several patterns can be found online. Students can color and cut from paper. Patterns have tabs that fold back and are taped so the dolls can stand on their own. By making several in various sizes, they can be nestled into each other. (See sample pattern in eResources online.)

Photograph by Mark Andrew Busch.

Recommended Read-Alouds

The picture books listed below are widely available in bookstores, libraries, and online. Although age guidelines are listed, the subject matter, illustrations, and cultural references offer ideal opportunities for discussion and learning for all elementary students and their families. For additional suggestions, please visit eResources online.

General

Amazing Faces, poems selected by Lee Bennett Hopkins, illustrated by Chris Soentpiet. Sixteen poems illustrated with faces of diverse children convey universal emotions. Ages 5 and up.

Around Our Way on Neighbors' Day, by Tameka Fryer Brown, illustrated by Charlotte Riley-Webb. Neighbors in an urban setting enjoy a summer block party in this toe-tapping, finger-snapping story. Ages 5–8.

Goal!, written by Sean Taylor, illustrated by Caio Vilela. Celebrates the worldwide love of soccer and shows how it is played around the globe. Photographs. Ages 5–11+.

I Am the World, by Charles R. Smith Jr. Photographs depict children of the world; accompanied by uplifting verse. Ages 5–10+.

Laundry Day, by Maurie J. Manning. Celebrating diversity in an urban neighborhood, this story follows a young boy who makes friends along his way. Ages 5–7.

The Immigrant Experience

Here I Am, by Patti Kim, illustrated by Sonia Sánchez. A boy new to urban America finds his way amid strange words, activities, and foods while finding comfort in a keepsake from his home country. Ages 5–7.

My Name Is Yoon, by Helen Recorvits, illustrated by Gabi Swiatkowska. Moving story with evocative illustrations chronicles a young Korean girl's assimilation into a new country.

Sumi's First Day of School Ever, by Soyung Pak, illustrated by Joung Un Kim. Sumi's first day of kindergarten in America is upsetting until she makes a friend. Ages 5–7.

Nations/Cultures Listed Alphabetically by Continent

Africa

My Grandfather Is a Magician: Work and Wisdom in an African Village, by Ifeoma Onyefulu. Depicts young boy's life in Nigeria and his grandfather's use of plants to heal. Ages 4–8.

Cameroon

The Market Bowl, by Jim Averbeck. A young girl in modern Cameroon tries to sell her unappetizing stew at the market and learns about integrity. Ages 4–8.

Egypt

The Day of Ahmed's Secret, by Florence Parry Heide and Judith Heide Gilliland, illustrated by Ted Lewin. A young boy must complete his job of delivering gas to the streetlamps before he can race home to tell his family his big news. Ages 5–8.

Ghana

One Hen: How One Small Loan Made a Big Difference, by Katie Smith Milway, illustrated by Eugenie Fernandes. An internationally acclaimed tale based on the true story of Kwabena Darko, a poultry farmer in Ghana, who, with the aid of a small loan, was able to grow his farm to employ 650 villagers. In turn, he extended loans to other small business owners throughout his community. Ages 8–12.

Kenya

Wangari's Trees of Peace: A True Story from Africa, by Jeanette Winter. Story of environmentalist and Nobel Peace Prize winner, Wangari Maathai. Ages 6–8.

South Africa

Abiyoyo, by Pete Seeger, illustrated by Michael Hays. A father and son, who often annoy the townspeople, save their village from Abiyoyo, the horrible giant. Ages 4–8.

Zimbabwe

Mufaro's Beautiful Daughters, by John Steptoe. The king, intending to choose among Mufaro's beautiful daughters, uses disguises to determine the true nature of each of the girls; Caldecott Honor. Ages 4–8.

Asia

Afghanistan
Afghan Dreams: Young Voices of Afghanistan, by Tony O'Brien and Mike Sullivan, photographs by Tony O'Brien. The faces and words of young Afghans who wish for peace. Ages 7–11+.

Bengal
Buri and the Marrow, by Hanriette Barkow, illustrated by Lizzie Finlay. In this folk tale, an old woman travels to see her daughter and must outwit several animals who wish to eat her. Ages 4–8.

China
Dancing to Freedom: The True Story of Mao's Last Dancer, by Li Cunxin, illustrated by Anne Spudvilas. Memoir of a poor boy who became a world-renowned dancer. Ages 7–10.

Hmong
Dia's Story Cloth, by Dia Cha. A story cloth tells the history of the Hmong people and the author's family. Ages 7+.

India
Elephant Dance: A Journey to India, by Theresa Henie, illustrated by Sheila Moxley. Ravi and Anjal welcome their grandfather from India and marvel at stories of his homeland. Ages 5–10.

Iraq
The Librarian of Basra: A True Story from Iraq, by Jeanette Winter. During the Iraqi war, Alia Muhammed Baker saved over 30,000 books and helped rebuild the library once the fighting ceased. Ages 7–9.

Japan
Coco-Chan's Kimono, by Kumiko Sudo. A young girl discovers nature outside her window as she waits for her mother to sew her new kimono. Ages 5–7.

Korea
The Firekeeper's Son, by Linda Sue Park, illustrated by Julie Downing. When his father is hurt, Sang-Hee must light the fire himself. Ages 4–8.

Laos
Dia's Story Cloth, by Dia Cha. See **Hmong**.

Pakistan

Nadia's Hands, by Karen English, illustrated by Jonathan Weiner. When a young Pakistani-American girl is asked to be in her aunt's wedding and her hands are decorated with *mehndi*, she is afraid of what her classmates will say when she returns to school. Ages 5–8.

Palestine

Sitti and the Cats: A Tale of Friendship, by Sally Bahous Allen, illustrated by Nancy Malick. A woman who befriends a talking cat is handsomely rewarded for her kindness. Ages 6–9.

Philippines

Tuko and the Birds, by Shirley Climo, illustrated by Francisco Mora. Everyone on the island knows it is time to sleep when they hear the birds' songs. When a noisy gecko arrives, no one can sleep until the eagle comes to the rescue. Ages 4–9.

Thailand

Dia's Story Cloth, by Dia Cha. See **Hmong**.

Turkey

A Donkey Reads, by Muriel Mandell, illustrated by André Letria. A tyrant becomes angry over a worthless offering. The villager who is to be punished is saved by a wise man who advises the tyrant he can teach the donkey to read. Ages 5+.

Vietnam

Tam and Cami: The Ancient Vietnamese Cinderella Story, by Minh Quoc, illustrated by Mai Long. Vietnamese version of Cinderella. Ages 6+.

Australia

Pheasant and Kingfisher, retold by Catherine H. Berndt, illustrated by Arone Raymond Meeks. Two men escape danger by turning into birds; an Aboriginal myth that explains how these birds came to be. Includes Aboriginal art. Ages 6+.

Central and South America

Gracias, Thanks, by Pat Mora, illustrated by John Parra. With text in English and Spanish, in this book a young boy gives thanks for everyday wonders. Ages 5–7.

Caribbean

Caribbean Dream, by Rachel Isadora. A typical day in the life of children on an island in the Caribbean; told in simple phrases and soft watercolors. Ages 3–7.

Chile

the composition, by Antonio Skármeta, illustrated by Alphonso Ruano. Pedro and his friends are more concerned about their soccer skills than politics until the dictatorship in Chile begins to affect them. Ages 8–12.

Guatemala

Sawdust Carpets, by Ameila Lau Carling. A young girl who watches her neighbors make a beautifully patterned "carpet" of sawdust becomes upset when she learns it is to be purposely destroyed during the Easter procession. Ages 5–9.

Honduras

The Good Garden: How One Family Went from Hunger to Having Enough, by Katie Smith Milway, illustrated by Sylvie Daigneault. The story of how changes in farming methods can lead to food security, a global issue for poor farmers. Ages 8–12.

Mexico

Bean Soup, by Jorge Argueta, illustrated by Rafael Yockteng. A young boy leaves his video games to help make a family comfort-food. A recipe in free verse. Ages 4–8.

Europe

Austria

A Gift for Mama, by Linda Ravin Lodding, illustrated by Alison Jay. Oskar's quest for a gift for his mother takes him through Vienna, portrayed in the beautiful artwork. Ages 4–8.

Czechoslovakia

The Wall: Growing Up Behind the Iron Curtain, by Peter Sis. Memoir of an award-winning children's author/illustrator. Ages 8–10.

Eastern Europe

Stories of Hope & Spirit: Folktales of Eastern Europe, by Dan Keding. Twelve folktales from various regions of Europe, such as Croatia, Romania, and Prussia. Ages 8–12.

Ireland

Miss Bridie Chose a Shovel, by Leslie Connor, illustrated by Mary Azarian. A young woman's shovel helps her transition to life in America. Ages 5–7.

Italy

All the Way to America: The Story of a Big Italian Family and a Little Shovel, by Dan Yaccarino. Based on the author/illustrator's family. Ages 4–7.

Russia

Kolobok, by Nataska Bochkov. Traditional Russian folktale similar to the Little Gingerbread Man. Ages 3–7.

Ukraine

The Mitten, by Jan Brett. In this well-known Ukrainian tale, forest animals make good use of a lost mitten. Ages 4–8.

North America

African American

All Different Now: Juneteenth, the First Day of Freedom, by Angela Johnson, illustrated by E. B. Lewis. Story of the day the last slaves in the South were emancipated; evocative watercolor illustrations. Ages 7–10.

Canada

Eskimo

Very Last First Time, by Jan Andrews, illustrated by Ian Wallace. A young girl who often helps her family collect mussels must complete this task by herself. Ages 5–9.

Native American

The Christmas Coat: Memories of My Sioux Childhood, by Virginia Driving Hawk Sneve, illustrated by Ellen Beier. Affecting tale based on the author's childhood; American Indian Youth Literature Award. Ages 6–9.

World Religions

Christianity

They Followed A Bright Star, based on a poem by Joan Alavedra, illustrated by Ulises Wensell. The story of those who followed the star, and those who remained behind to participate each in their way in the coming of Baby Jesus. Ages 5–7.

Islam

Celebrating Ramadan, by Diane Hoyt-Goldsmith, illustrated by Lawrence Migdale. A boy living in America shares his knowledge of the Islamic faith and the celebration of Ramadan. Ages 8+.

The Swirling Hijaab, by Na'ima Bint Robert, illustrated by Nilesh Mistry. A young girl uses her imagination as she tries on her mother's hijaab. As she plays with it, she also realizes its importance in her faith. Ages 5–9.

Judaism

New Year at the Pier: A Rosh Hashanah Story, by April Halprin Wayland, illustrated by Stephane Jorisch. A family prepares for Tashlich, the Jewish New Year ceremony; lyrical text and appealing art. Ages 5–8.

An extensive list of additional Read-Aloud Recommendations can be found in eResources online.

Craft and Multicultural Book Sources

- Asia for Kids, accessed June 27, 2014, www.afk.com/catalog/entry.tpl
- Culture for Kids, accessed June 2014, www.cultureforkids.com/
- DLTK, accessed June 27, 2014, www.dltk-kids.com/world/index.htm
- Kids.gov, accessed June 27, 2014, http://kids.usa.gov/social-studies/countries-and-cultures
- Language Lizard, accessed June 27, 2014, www.languagelizard.com/
- Mantralingua, accessed June 27, 2014, http://usa.mantralingua.com/
- Pinterest, accessed June 27, 2014, www.pinterest.com/4thrprogram/kids-multicultural-arts-crafts/

Bibliography

Alba, Richard and Victor Nee, "Rethinking Assimilation Theory for a New Era of Immigration," special issue, *International Migration Review* 31, no. 4 (Winter 1997): 826–874.

Berry, John. W., "Immigration, Acculturation and Adaptation," *Applied Psychology: An International Review* 46, no. 1 (1997): 5–68.

Brand, Susan Trostle and Laurie J. Harper, "More Alike Than Different: Promoting Respect Through Multicultural Books and Literacy Strategies," *Childhood Education* 86, no. 4 (Summer 2010): 224–233.

Conzen, Kathleen Neils, David A. Gerber, Ewa Morawska, George E. Pozzetta, and Rudolph J. Vecoli, "The Invention of Ethnicity: A Perspective from the U.S.A.," *Journal of American Ethnic History* 12, no. 1 (Fall 1992): 3–41.

Gay, Geneva, *Culturally Responsive Teaching: Theory, Research, and Practice*. New York: Teachers College Press, 2000.

Glazier, Jocelyn and Jung-A Seo, "Multicultural Literature and Discussion as Mirror and Window?" *Journal of Adolescent & Adult Literacy* 48, no. 8 (May 2005): 686–700, doi:10.1598/JAAL.48.8.6

Gordon, Milton Myron, *Assimilation in American Life*. New York: Oxford University Press, 1964.

"Immigration Act of 1990," Pub. L. 101–649, 101st Congress, accessed June 27, 2014, www.justice.gov/eoir/IMMACT1990.pdf

McDonald, Hellen G. and Pallassana R. Balgopal, "Conflicts of American Immigrants: Assimilate or Retain Ethnic Identity," *Migration World Magazine* 26 no. 4 (May/June 1998): 14–19.

Vigdor, Jacob L., "Measuring Immigrant Assimilation in Post-Recession America," Manhattan Institute for Policy Research Civic Report 76 (March 2013), accessed June 27, 2014, www.manhattan-institute.org/html/cr_76.htm#.U63EE0CwX4Q

Part V

Year-End Parent/Caregiver Literacy Booster Meeting

CHAPTER 11

School's Out! Now What?
Ideas for Minimizing the "Summer Slide"

As the school year winds down, educators and students eagerly anticipate the more relaxed schedule that summer vacation affords. However, a lengthy school break can result in a decline of one to three months in language arts and mathematics achievement scores (Cooper et al. 1996). Studies have shown that this "summer slide" most affects elementary students of low socioeconomic status (Alexander et al. 2001) and continues to affect those students beyond high school as they enter post-secondary education or the job market (Alexander et al. 2007).

To temper this decline, some schools now maintain a year-round academic calendar that minimizes lengthy vacations. Many school districts offer summer remediation or enrichment programs. Parents/caregivers of mid or high socioeconomic status may seek private tutors, summer camp experiences, or academic day care programs for their children. Such programs may not be feasible financially or logistically for some families. As a result, during school breaks children may increase their screen time, engaging in video gaming, television viewing, and computer and tablet activities. Use of such electronic devices has been increasing (American Academy of Child and Adolescent Psychiatry 2011; Common Sense Media 2013) and can result in obesity, behavioral problems, learning difficulties, and sleep disorders (Ozmert et al. 2002; Landhuis, et al. 2007). Students can and should be engaged in learning activities each day during school breaks to maintain and extend the knowledge and skills they acquire in the classroom.

This Literacy Booster Meeting will share with parents/caregivers insights and resources that encourage them to provide children with enjoyable and motivating learning opportunities to minimize the "summer slide" over school vacations.

Susan E. Busch. Photograph used with permission.

School's Out! Now What?

Grade Levels: K–5

Time: 1.5 hours

Supplies
- Large room with tables and chairs to seat all comfortably
- Chart paper/whiteboard and markers
- Copies of Resource Packet
- Read-aloud book

- Document reader, opaque projector, or another means for sharing the read-aloud book
- Pamphlets from local stores and cultural institutions
- A list of area educational attractions with addresses, website links, and fees

Activity materials
- A selection of fresh leaves from a variety of trees
- Pencils and unlined paper
- Two or more unusual fruits or vegetables (e.g., Ugli fruit, edamame, kiwi)
- Information about produce from store displays
- Light refreshments (optional)

Goals
- Participants will engage in easy, low-cost activities that reinforce important learning skills.
- Participants will be introduced to resources for planning summer learning activities for students.
- Participants will become familiar with local places to visit with children.
- Participants will plan several vacation learning opportunities.

Literacy Booster Meeting Planning

Several weeks in advance
- ❑ Select the date and reserve a large room.
- ❑ Research and prepare a list of local trips. (See form in Resource Packet.)
- ❑ Prepare a calendar of the summer months. (See form in Resource Packet.)
- ❑ Arrange for publicity through the school website and calendar, classroom calendars, announcements, and through the school parent organization.
- ❑ Collect informative flyers and pamphlets from area stores (regarding produce, services, and products), cultural institutions, and recreation facilities; collect children's books. (See Recommended Read-Aloud list in Resource Packet.)
- ❑ Arrange for childcare room and transportation, if provided; solicit volunteers to staff (optional).
- ❑ As event draws near, send home an invitation to all families. Include a registration form to enable preparation of the room and ensure ample materials. (See registration form in Resource Packet.)

One week in advance
- ❑ Confirm room.
- ❑ Send reminder to families.
- ❑ Confirm childcare and transportation arrangements, if applicable.
- ❑ Practice the read-aloud. Model the read-aloud behaviors you hope to foster in participants.

❑ Prepare copies of the Resource Packet.

❑ Prepare the Family Trip Suggestion chart by researching local destinations for family outings. Try to choose venues within a day's drive. Leave blank spaces for participants' suggestions.

Suggested venues include:
- Airports
- Art galleries and museums
- Bookstores that offer free children's clubs and events
- Children's museums
- Historical societies or museums
- Lakes and public ponds
- National, state, and local parks
- Nature preserves
- Naval parks and historical forts
- Public historical buildings
- Recreational areas
- Science museums
- Unusual land formations
- U-pick farms
- Utility displays
- Zoos

The day of the event

❑ Set up the room. Display flyers, pamphlets, and children's books.

❑ Organize Resource Packets and activity materials for easy access.

❑ Greet participants as they arrive. Distribute Resource Packets and invite participants to browse the tables and enjoy refreshments.

Leading the Literacy Booster Meeting

○ 5 minutes: **Begin promptly** with a warm welcome, a brief introduction of all staff present, a reminder to silence cell phones, and an explanation of the goals for the event. Circulate attendance sheet. Review location of restrooms and fire/emergency exit details.

○ **Talking Points**
- Although children look forward to summer vacations and winter and spring breaks, they can lose some skills and knowledge while away from their desks.
- Learning doesn't just happen in school.
- We can establish a culture of lifetime learning in our homes.
- Learning at home need not be structured or formal.
- Learning activities need not be expensive or time-consuming.
- Today we will look at excellent ways to learn during school breaks: In Our Own Backyard, In My Neighborhood, and Family Trips.

○ 10 minutes: **Read aloud** *A Fine, Fine School*, by Sharon Creech, illustrated by Harry Bliss. Ask:

- What were some of the things the children were studying?
- What were the children learning over weekends, vacations, and holidays?
- What other learning activities do children experience over weekends, holidays, and vacations?

○ 10 minutes: **In Our Own Backyard Part 1**

- Distribute to each person: a sheet of white paper, a pencil, and a leaf.
- Direct participants to place the leaf under the paper and lightly scribble over it. This is a leaf rubbing.
- Ask participants to compare their rubbings with a person near them. How are they alike? How are they different? From what kind of tree might this leaf come? Where can we find that information? (books on trees, nurseries, Internet)
- Ask the group how this activity might motivate students.

○ 10 minutes: **In Our Own Backyard Part 2**

- Distribute another piece of paper to each participant.
- Ask them to draw a map of their yard.
- Discuss what might be included. (orientation, key, labels)
- Ask: How do these help us to better understand your map?
- Ask: What would your child learn by drawing a map? What maps could they create?

○ 10 minutes: **In Our Own Backyard Part 3**

- Turn to the first page of the Resource Packet for suggested activities parents/caregivers and children can do at home during school breaks.
- Read through the activities. Ask for additional suggestions. List on chart paper/whiteboard.
- See also the select list of websites offering activities.

Photograph by Mark Andrew Busch.

○ 15 minutes: **In My Neighborhood**
- Hold up an unusual fruit or vegetable. Ask:
- Does anyone know what this is? I found it at the grocery store.
- Where can we find information about this kind of produce?
- Tell a bit about the produce if no one offers information. Share information the store provided.
- Continue with other fruits or vegetables as time allows.
- Ask: What can your child learn about these fruits and vegetables? (where they are grown, other plants to which they are related, how they can be prepared)
- Ask where they can learn about them. (store, books, Internet)
- Turn to In My Neighborhood in the Resource Packet.
- Read through the activities. Ask for additional suggestions. List on chart paper/ whiteboard.

Susan E. Busch. Used with permission.

○ 15 minutes: **Take a Trip**
  • Ask participants to name a favorite family trip or outing. List on chart paper/whiteboard.
  • Ask: What was interesting or unusual?
  • Ask: What did your children learn on the trip or outing?
  • Refer to Family Trip Suggestions in Resource Packet.
  • Briefly describe each listing.
  • Add places suggested by participants.
○ 15 minutes: **Closing the Literacy Booster Meeting**
  • Turn to the calendar page. Explain that participants now have time to do some planning.
  • Encourage participants to take a few moments to read over the ideas, thinking about their children's interests and ages. Suggest that they write on the calendar page a few activities they would like to do with their children over school break.
  • Note the list of recommended books with themes related to vacations and places to visit in the Resource Packet and displayed on the table.
  • Ask if there are any questions.
  • Ask participants to complete a brief evaluation of the meeting in order to offer valuable feedback for future meetings. (See Appendix for an example of an evaluation form.)
  • Thank volunteers and participants for attending.
  • Transfer ideas and suggestions noted on chart paper/whiteboard onto a follow-up sheet that can be sent home or included in a future communication.

Gene Bradbury. Used with permission.

Bibliography

Alexander, Karl L., Doris R. Entwisle, and Linda S. Olsen, "Lasting Consequences of the Summer Learning Gap," *American Sociological Review* 72, no. 2 (April 2007): 167–180, doi:10.1177/000312240707200202

Alexander, Karl L., Doris R. Entwisle, and Linda S. Olsen, "Schools, Achievement, and Inequality: A Seasonal Perspective," *Educational Evaluation and Policy Analysis* 23, no. 2 (Summer 2001): 171–191, doi:10.3102/01623737023002171

American Academy of Child and Adolescent Psychiatry, "Children and Watching TV," Facts for Families Pages no. 54 (December 2011), accessed August 11, 2014, www.aacap.org/AACAP/Families_and_Youth/Facts_for_Families/Facts_for_Families_Pages/Children_And_Wat_54.aspx

Common Sense Media, "Zero to Eight: Children's Media Use in America," October 2013, accessed August 11, 2014, www.commonsensemedia.org/sites/default/files/research/zerotoeightfinal2011.pdf

Cooper, Harris, Barbara Nye, Kelly Charlton, James Lindsay, and Scott Greathouse, "The Effects of Summer Vacation on Achievement Test Scores: A Narrative and Meta-analytic Review," *Review of Educational Research* 66, no. 3 (Fall 1996): doi:10.3102/00346543066003227

Landhuis, Carl Erik, Richie Poulton, David Welch, and Robert John Hancox, "Does Childhood Television Viewing Lead to Attention Problems in Adolescence: Results from a Prospective Longitudinal Study," *Pediatrics* 120, no. 3 (September 2007): doi:10.1542/peds.2007–0978

Ozmert, Elif, Muge Toyran, and Kadriye Yurdakok, "Behavioral Correlates of Television Viewing in Primary School Children Evaluated by the Child Behavior Checklist," *Archives of Pediatrics and Adolescent Medicine* 156, no. 9 (September 2002): 910–914, doi: 10.1001/archpedi.156.9.910

Resource Packet for School's Out! Now What? can be found on the following pages. See also related Take-Home TipSheet in Chapter 12. TipSheets in color and in Spanish can be found in eResources online.

Worried that your children will forget what they have learned in school this year?
Looking for ways to keep them learning during vacation?

Come join us!

School's Out! Now What?

Keep 'Em Learning This Summer!

_____
Date and time

_____
Place

Please return registration form by

_____
Date

Yes, I/we will attend **School's Out! Now What?**

Parent(s)/Caregiver(s) _____

Teacher _____ Room _____

Number of adults attending _____

Number of children for childcare _____

School's Out! Now What?
Parent/Caregiver Resource Packet

Activity Ideas: In My Own Backyard

1. **Read. Read. Read.** Create a home library! Use a sturdy cardboard box set on its side. Collect books, magazines, newspapers, materials sent home by the school, and even food cartons or bags. Trade books with friends. Make a colorful chart in the shape of a soccer field or the solar system. Kids can use a soccer ball or space ship made from a sticky note to track the number of pages read, moving the marker across the field or solar system. Be sure to discuss books they are reading.

2. **Take a walk outside.** Discover insects living beneath rocks. Study the design of a spider web. Keep a list of the kinds of trees, flowers, or birds you see in your yard. Watch and discuss the seasonal changes in plants and animals.

3. **Plant a garden.** Seeds are inexpensive. Growing vegetables may encourage children to try new foods. If you do not have access to a plot of land, make a container garden. Use a pail, recycle a plastic trash can—or even a fabric tote will do. Encourage children to take responsibility for

Susan E. Busch. Used with permission.

watering, weeding, and harvesting the garden. Discuss changes as plants grow.

4. **Weather station.** Using a black permanent marker, make ¼ inch marks on a clear jar to construct a rain gauge. A 2" by 12" strip of fabric glued or taped on one end of a yard stick makes a wind vane. Purchase an inexpensive thermometer. Place all three instruments in an open area. Collect data each day. Research the various types of cloud formations and their properties. Your meteorologist can offer the family a daily weather report!

Mark Andrew Busch. Used with permission.

Mark Andrew Busch. Used with permission.

5. **Track sports statistics.** Student athletes can keep track of their statistics: game scores, practices, and skill improvement. Graph statistics of favorite teams or players.

6. **Keep a family journal.** Family members can take turns writing about their day in a shared notebook. Focus on the best thing and the hardest thing that happens each day. Share and discuss ways to react or cope with difficult events. Celebrate happy moments.

7. **Vacation scrapbook.** Children can keep a notebook of pictures and artifacts from their summer experiences. Discuss items and write captions that explain experiences.

8. **Family game night.** Gather the family and enjoy regularly scheduled game nights. Discuss strategy and personal reactions while playing. Help children learn sportsmanship, following directions and rules, and even reading and math skills.

Stephen Truitt. Used with permission.

9. **Plan and prepare a meal.** When children plan and assist in preparing a meal they learn about nutrition, where food comes from, measurement, and how to read recipes, and they gain an appreciation for food preparation. Children also learn self-sufficiency and independent living skills. Food prep often increases the variety of foods children will eat.

10. **Websites:**
    - www.sciencebob.com/index.php
    - http://nickandtesla.com/
    - www.familyeducation.com/

Activity Ideas: In My Neighborhood

1. **Grocery store.** Visit the produce section. Read labels and any information or recipes the store provides. Visit the seafood department or the butcher. Encourage your child to ask questions about various items and their origins. Read information on food packaging.

2. **Plant or flower shop.** Visit a nursery or flower shop. Read labels to learn about plant care. Ask questions such as: How do you pronounce the name of this plant? What does annual, bi-annual, and perennial mean? What does fertilizer do?

3. **Construction site.** Look for road work, building construction, or remodeling sites. Keep a safe distance but watch the progression of the project. Visit over several days. Discuss what is happening, the names of the construction vehicles or tools, and how construction will improve the area.

4. **Architecture tour.** Leave the cell phone at home or turn it off and take a walk around your neighborhood. Talk about the buildings. Note the type of architecture. Does the style have a name? Look at trees and plants. How has the neighborhood changed since you moved there? What would you like to see added to the neighborhood?

5. **Make a map of your neighborhood.** Try to draw to scale. What can you use to measure? How are buildings numbered? How does that help people find what they're looking for?

6. **Signs.** Point out signs in the neighborhood (sale, political, traffic, ads). Note vocabulary. For example: yield and merge. What do they mean? How are they the same? Different? Discuss business names.

7. **Cemetery.** Walking in a cemetery might seem strange, but it is often quiet and can lead to discussion. Headstone inscriptions can lead to information about historical events.

8. **Specialty shops.** Visit a neighborhood specialty shop, such as an ethnic food store, independent bookstore, or dry cleaner. Find a time when they

may not be busy. Most owners are happy to talk about their business. Encourage your child to ask questions.

9. **Library.** Visit your neighborhood library often. Help your child sign up for a library card. Explore books, magazines, e-books, and computers. Read notices of community events.

10. **Playground.** Enjoy play time with your child. Which parts of the playground are favorites? Why? Discuss playground safety. What would you change or add to make the playground more interesting or fun?

Family Trip Suggestions

Place	Address	Cost

It is a happy talent to know how to play.

—Ralph Waldo Emerson

Month:

Sunday	Monday	Tuesday	Wednesday	Thursday	Friday	Saturday

Month:

Sunday	Monday	Tuesday	Wednesday	Thursday	Friday	Saturday

Recommended Read-Alouds

A Is for America: An American Alphabet, by Devin Scillian, illustrated by Pam Carroll. Written in rhyme, this alphabet book depicts fascinating people, places, and items important in the history of the United States. Ages 6–10.

All the World, by Liz Garton Scanlon, illustrated by Marla Frazee. This glimpse of a summer day along the coastline ends with the uplifting lines, "Hope and peace and love and trust/All the world is all of us." Ages 4–7.

A Beach Day, by Douglas Florian. A tribute to a day at the beach is filled with jubilant poetry. Ages 3–6.

Beach Day, by Karen Roosa, illustrated by Maggie Smith. Lyrical look at a fun day; aptly illustrated in watercolor. Ages 3–5.

Blueberries for Sal, by Robert McCloskey. A perfect read-aloud for a day of berry-picking. Ages 3–7.

A Fine, Fine School, by Sharon Creech, illustrated by Harry Bliss. Principal Keene is so proud of the learning the students engage in each day he decides to extend the school year. Tillie reminds Mr. Keene that kids learn when they aren't in school, and the principal restores the traditional calendar. Ages 5–8.

Growing Vegetable Soup, by Lois Ehlert. Bright, bold, engaging look at raising vegetables. See also: *Eating the Alphabet: Fruits & Vegetables from A to Z*. Ages 4–7.

Have Fun, Molly Lou Melon, by Patty Lovell, illustrated by David Catrow. Grandma teaches Molly Lou, who in turn shows her new friend that an active imagination is the best thing for having fun. Ages 6–8.

How I Spent My Summer Vacation, by Mark Teague. Wallace uses his impressive imagination to embellish an essay about his summer vacation. Ages 5–8.

In the Tree House, by Andrew Larsen, illustrated by Dušan Petričić. Two brothers enjoy each other's company in their tree house during a power outage. Ages 5–8.

Kimo's Summer Vacation, by Kerry Germain, illustrated by Keoni Montes. Kimo learns it's possible to have exciting adventures in his own backyard. Ages 5–8.

The Night Before Summer Vacation, by Natasha Wing, illustrated by Julie Durrell. Told in the style of the famous Christmas poem, this humorous story tells about a family packing for a camping trip. Ages 3–7.

Sailaway Home, by Bruce Degen. A toy sailboat launches adventures in independence in this rhyming tale. Ages 3–6.

Part VI

Additional Teacher Resources

CHAPTER 12

Take-Home TipSheets

Sending home brief, eye-catching literacy tips on a regular basis reinforces and extends strategies discussed at Literacy Booster Meetings or experienced at Family Literacy Events. Keep literacy on parents' and caregivers' minds with "Sharing Our Secrets" Take-Home TipSheets that offer quick tips, book recommendations, websites of interest to children, and a bounty of creative ways to boost learning. Copy-ready and suitable for stuffing in backpacks, Take-Home TipSheets strengthen the home–school connection. Plan to send them home often!

The Take-Home TipSheets are available in color and in Spanish in eResources online.

Pssst! We're Sharing Our Secrets!

Quick Tips for School Success

Fill in the blanks to find a surefire path to SCHOOL SUCCESS:

RE__D TO Y__UR CH__LD.

Reading aloud is the **single most important thing** you can do to improve your child's attitude toward reading. And this doesn't mean reading only to your toddler. Read aloud to your middle grader and preteen, too! Never read to your kid? Stopped reading aloud when your child learned to read? No worries! **It's not too late!** These simple tips will kick-start the read-aloud habit and keep it going strong! **Book on!**

1. Choose books together. Find something to read aloud that appeals to both of you. Look for books that make you laugh, or tremble, or sigh. If you love the book, your child will get that—and also get that **reading is fun.**
2. **Read aloud every day.**
3. Before you read to your child, look through the book or chapter so you know what's coming. This helps you **read with expression.** When a character is worried, make your voice quiver. When the story is spooky, *whisper*. When something silly happens, share a giggle-laugh-hoot! Take time to enjoy the pictures. Draw older children in with the first sentence or paragraph and make the last line a cliffhanger. Your child will be begging you not to stop reading and will be reaching for the book the next day. Good, good, good, because **we're forming a habit here. We. Read. Every. Day.**
4. Find a comfy, quiet spot to enjoy your daily read-aloud. **You and your child will look forward to and treasure this special time together.**

Working Together to Strengthen Literacy and the Home–School Connection

Literacy Is  Powerful!

Pssst! We're Sharing Our Secrets!
Quick Tips: "Wrap It Up!" Recap

At our **"Wrap It Up!"** event we explored ways to support learning by choosing gifts that teach while they entertain. We discovered the fun and value of playing with our children, **talking together,** and **explaining our thinking and reasoning** while enjoying a game or solving a problem. We read a book, too, about what makes a gift special.

"Wrap It Up" Recap:

1. Start a **Family Game Night** tradition! Choose games that teach as well as entertain, and have lots of fun! **Ask your child to read the game rules or directions. Talk** together while playing. **"Think aloud"** strategies. **Explain** moves. **Encourage and model fair play and sportsmanship.**

2. Keep your child's **wish list** from our event handy when buying gifts.

3. The following books reinforce the idea that gifts and treasure need not be "things," and fun can be had without expensive toys or gadgets. **Read aloud** and **discuss** these stories. (See also books listed in "Wrap It Up" handout.)

   ❖ *Cheer Up, Mouse!*, by Jed Henry. Ages 4–7.
   ❖ *The Day It Rained Hearts*, by Felicia Bond. Ages 5–7.
   ❖ *Have Fun, Molly Lou Melon*, by Patty Lovell, illustrated by David Catrow. Ages 4–7.
   ❖ *Knots on a Counting Rope*, by Bill Martin Jr. and John Archambault, illustrated by Ted Rand. Ages 5–8.
   ❖ *A Sick Day for Amos McGee*, by Philip C. Stead, illustrated by Erin E. Stead. All ages.
   ❖ *Thank You, World*, by Alice B. McGinty, illustrated by Wendy Anderson Halperin. Ages 5–8.

Working Together to Strengthen Literacy and the Home–School Connection

Literacy Is  Powerful!

Pssst! We're Sharing Our Secrets!
Quick Tips: "School's Out!" Follow-Up

At our **"School's Out"** meeting we discussed the importance of keeping kids thinking and learning while enjoying summer vacation. Avoid the "summer slide" by helping your child maintain skills gained throughout the school year!

FUN To-do List:
✓ Make visiting the library a weekly habit. It's free!
✓ Explore your yard, your neighborhood, your community! Search for free events.

Marvelous! Fabulous! Outstanding! The Right Book at the Right Time
Marvelous! Must-Read Books for NEW readers beginning to read on their own:
○ *The Carrot Seed*, by Ruth Krauss, illustrated by Crockett Johnson.
○ **Cork & Fuzz** series, by Dori Chaconas, illustrated by Lisa McCue.
○ **Elephant & Piggie** books, by Mo Willems.
○ **Fly Guy** series, by Tedd Arnold.
○ **Henry and Mudge** series, by Cynthia Rylant.

Fabulous! Chapter Book Authors for 2nd–3rd grade readers:
○ Ann Cameron
○ Patricia Reilly Giff
○ Claudia Mills
○ Beverly Cleary
○ Joanna Hurwitz
○ Ann Whitehead Nagda

Outstanding! Authors of terrific books for 4th–5th grade readers:
○ Andrew Clements (many books!)
○ Eva Ibbotson (fantasy)
○ Sharon Creech (variety!)
○ Louis Sachar (more humor!)
○ Jack Gantos (humor boys love!)
○ Lemony Snicket (ditto!)

Note: Maturity, interests, and reading levels vary among children. Choose books accordingly.

Working Together to Strengthen Literacy and the Home–School Connection

Literacy Is  Powerful!

Pssst! We're Sharing Our Secrets!
Our Public Library: Free, Safe, and Fun!

WOW! The local public library and the larger regional library system are home to **stacks of terrific books** for children (and teens and adults). They also offer worthwhile programming from crafts to computers during school breaks.

Take advantage of this fabulous **free** community resource! Sign up for a **library card** for each of your children. Then start enjoying the place! Browse and sit awhile. Here are a handful of titles to look for. ***Read, dream, believe, achieve!***

Treasures on the Shelves: Books to Check Out (at the Library!)

Primary Grades:

Alfie Runs Away, by Kenneth M. Cadow
Bear Feels Scared; Bear Feels Sick, by Karma Wilson
A Day with Dad, by Bo R. Holmberg
Orange Pear Apple Bear, by Emily Gravett
Pssst!, by Adam Rex

Intermediate Grades:

A Long Walk to Water and other books by Linda Sue Park
The Underneath, by Kathi Appelt
Novels by Christopher Paul Curtis, Katherine Paterson, and Jacqueline Woodson

Note: Maturity, interests, and reading levels vary among children. Choose books accordingly.

Working Together to Strengthen Literacy and the Home–School Connection

Literacy Is  Powerful!

Pssst! We're Sharing Our Secrets!
Quick Tips: "Celebrating Us!" Follow-Up

At our **"Celebrating Us!"** event we enjoyed Culture Stations and sampled favorite dishes from across the world. We read stories, too, on a night that was a festive occasion to come together as a school family.

We encourage families to spend time together making the dishes you enjoyed at our event. Search online for the recipe. Ask your child to **read the recipe** and help you follow the steps. Interested in making additional crafts featured at our event? Ask your child to **read the list of materials** and help gather them. **Read the instructions** and enjoy creating something together!

These books celebrate diversity. Suitable to read aloud to children ages 4–8:
  Amazing Faces, poems selected by Lee Bennett Hopkins, illustrated by Chris Soentpiet
  Families, by Susan Kuklin
  Goal!, by Sean Taylor, illustrated by Caio Vilela
  If America Were a Village: A Book about the People of the United States, and If the World Were a Village: A Book about the World's People, by David J. Smith, illustrated by Shelagh Armstrong
  Laundry Day, by Maurie J. Manning
  Shades of People, by Shelley Rotner and Sheila M. Kelly
  Thank You, World, by Alice B. McGinty, illustrated by Wendy Anderson Halperin

Explore other cultures! These books are suitable to read aloud to children ages 9–12:
  A Long Walk to Water, by Linda Sue Park
  Parched, by Melanie Crowder
  Same Sun Here, Silas House and Neela Vaswani
  Serafina's Promise, by Ann E. Burg

Note: Maturity, interests, and reading levels vary among children. Choose books accordingly.

Working Together to Strengthen Literacy and the Home–School Connection

Literacy Is  Powerful!

Pssst! We're Sharing Our Secrets!
Series are Seriously FUN ... and a gateway to wider reading!

Kids like having friends. And when they meet someone they feel comfortable with, they look forward to spending time together. So, it only makes sense that kids enjoy reading books in series: They know the characters, feel comfortable in their world, and look forward to spending time with them. That means more time with BOOKS, and as kids discover that reading is fun, they'll look for more friends in books!

Introduce young readers to these characters:

- **Clementine** series and **Stuart** series, by Sara Pennypacker
- **Goofballs** series, by Tony Abbott
- **Horrible Harry** series, by Suzy Kline
- **Magic Tree House** series, by Mary Pope Osborne
- **Nikki & Deja** series, by Karen English, illustrated by Laura Freeman
- **Polk Street School** series, by Patricia Reilly Giff
- **Ramona** series, by Beverly Cleary
- **Riverside Kids** series, by Johanna Hurwitz
- *The Stories Julian Tells,* and other titles by Ann Cameron, illustrated by Ann Strugnell

Introduce middle grade readers to these books:

- **Chet Gecko Mystery** series, by Bruce Hale
- **Diary of a Wimpy Kid** series, by Jeff Kinney
- **Girls to the Rescue** series, edited by Bruce Lansky
- **Goddess Girls** series, by Joan Holub
- **Guys Read** series, edited by Jon Scieszka
- **Hazardous Tales** series, by Nathan Hale
- **Joey Pigza** books, by Jack Gantos
- **Lunch Lady** series, by Jarrett J. Krosoczka
- **World of Adventure** series, by Gary Paulsen

Note: Maturity, interests, and reading levels vary among children. Choose books accordingly.

Working Together to Strengthen Literacy and the Home–School Connection

Literacy Is  Powerful!

Pssst! We're Sharing Our Secrets!
Quick Tips: "Organize It!" Follow-Up

At our **"Organize It!"** event we shared ways to help children feel successful at managing their time and completing homework and other responsibilities. Let's recap the highlights of our discussions:

→ **Routine** is important for all of us. Children feel secure and get comfort from routines, and though they may complain at times, a schedule makes it easier for you to set expectations and meet goals.

→ A **homework contract** is an excellent means for avoiding arguments with older children. Once you discuss your child's responsibilities and put expectations in writing, there will be fewer disagreements and less chance for kids to try to avoid doing what needs to get done. Keep the homework contract in a handy spot and refer to it when necessary! Be consistent!

→ A **timer** is an excellent tool to develop attention span. It sets an expectation that a certain amount of time will be devoted to a specific task—and also helps children see that there is a limit to the time they must spend on a task. Set reasonable amounts of times for tasks to be completed. Know your child's limits. Breaks are helpful; build them into the schedule. If work isn't finished when the timer dings, calmly discuss why. Work with your child and, if necessary, your child's teacher to find a solution.

→ Homework can be more fun with nifty pens, jazzy markers, neon pencils, and organizers, such as *The Wimpy Kid School Planner.* Keep supplies in a handy spot. Find a **quiet, brightly lit** area with **few distractions.** Turn off the TV and other media. Be encouraging. Keep an eye on progress and supervise—from a distance.

Working Together to Strengthen Literacy and the Home–School Connection

Literacy Is  Powerful!

Pssst! We're Sharing Our Secrets!
Quick Tips: "A Night Out with the Guys" Follow-Up

At our **"A Night Out with the Guys"** event, we enjoyed an evening focused on entertainment—and learning—with the boys. We shared ideas for picking up skills while having fun together and looked at books that are sure to add to read-aloud enjoyment in the home. Let's recap:

- ☑ You are a hero in your child's eyes. In fact, your child learns simply by watching you! So be a GREAT role model! Learning takes place even when you play with your child. Help your child read and follow directions, learn how to take turns, and count. Show your child how to win—and how to lose. It's a skill!
- ☑ When your child sees you reading, it becomes more valuable. Remember, you're the role model. Be a reading hero!
- ☑ Discuss what you read together. Talk about the story—relate it to personal experiences you or your child has had. Discuss what you learn in a factual book or article. Help your child see the connection between books and life.
- ☑ Sharing time together builds relationships. Put away your cell phone. Turn off the TV and other media and spend time talking and playing with your child.
- ☑ Ask your child questions about things that are important to him. Encourage him to share thoughts and feelings. Share your experiences as a child with similar problems or concerns. Discuss solutions and lend support.
- ☑ Let your child teach you something new! Be enthusiastic and praise his knowledge and skill.

Working Together to Strengthen Literacy and the Home–School Connection

Literacy Is  Powerful!

Pssst! We're Sharing Our Secrets!
What Does That Mean??
A Key to Teacher Lingo

Educators have special words and abbreviations that stand for things common to their work, just as plumbers, electricians, doctors, engineers, landscapers, salespeople, and workers in most every line of work do. Yet sometimes it's confusing trying to figure out just what we're talking about! Here is just a handful of common teacher-terms so you can feel more comfortable if we forget and lapse into Teacher-ese!

- ❖ **PTA/PTO—The Parent Teacher Association**—our link to working together for the good of the school. Get involved! We need you.
- ❖ **ELLs**—English Language Learners—those among us who are learning to speak, read, write, and understand American English.

  - ❖ **Common Core State Standards**—national and state expectations for learning and achievement from Pre-K through high school. Sometimes called CCSS or Common Core.
  - ❖ **ELA—English Language Arts**—areas of learning that include listening, speaking, reading, and writing. In high school this is commonly called English.

- ❖ **Fluency**—There's more to fluency than reading fast. Think of it as fluid—reading with natural pauses, and most of all, with understanding. Fluency is not speed reading, but careful reading at a good pace, without halting or struggling so much that understanding is affected.

Remember, it's fine to ask me at any time, "What does that mean?"

Working Together to Strengthen Literacy and the Home–School Connection

Literacy Is  Powerful!

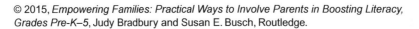

Pssst! We're Sharing Our Secrets!
Quick Clicks: Websites for Parents/Caregivers

These websites intended for parents and caregivers are worth exploring!

www.pbs.org/parents/education/reading-language/reading-activities/ http://pbskids.org/island/parents/

www.pbs.org/parents/readinglanguage/

www.rif.org/us/literacy-resources/articles.htm

www2.readaloud.org/importance?gclid=COPJ_N6ZmL8CFW4Q7AodHhkA3Q

www.readingfoundation.org/parents.jsp

www2.ed.gov/parents/read/resources/edpicks.jhtml

www.readingrockets.org/audience/parents

www.readwritethink.org/parent-afterschool-resources/

www.pageahead.org/childrens-literacy_tips-for-parents.php

www.kdl.org/kids/go/pgr_main

www.kdl.org/kids/go/pgr_development_activities

https://pals.virginia.edu/parents-monthly-activity.html

www.getreadytoread.org/early-learning-childhood-basics/early-literacy/promoting-family-literacy-raising-ready-readers

http://projectenlightenment.wcpss.net/parent_resources/early_literacy_tips.html

www.cal.org/caela/tools/program_development/elltoolkit/Part3-23LiteracyActivitiesintheHome.pdf

Internet addresses were accurate at time of publication.

Working Together to Strengthen Literacy and the Home-School Connection

Literacy Is  Powerful!

Pssst! We're Sharing Our Secrets!
Quick Clicks: Websites for Kids

Check out these fantastic, FUN, literacy-boosting websites with your children!

Perfect for Primary Grades:

www.curiousgeorge.com/ Curious George is at it again!

Made for Middle Graders:

https://newsela.com/ News kids can use.

http://smithsonianquests.org/ Projects and activities brought to you by the Smithsonian!

Something for Everyone:

www.funbrain.com/ Reading, Math, & Games galore! (A Parent's Page, too!)

http://wonderopolis.org/ A WONDER-full site offering tons of learning fun!

http://kids.nationalgeographic.com/ National Geographic Kids' site is awesome!

http://kids.albrightknox.org/loader.html Hosted by Buffalo, NY's Albright-Knox Art Gallery, this interactive site features art games in English and Spanish for ages 4–12.

Terrific Tip! Great Websites for Kids: http://gws.ala.org/ lists great sites by categories and recommends a "site of the week!" Sponsored by the American Library Association.

Always supervise your child's use of the Internet. *

Working Together to Strengthen Literacy and the Home–School Connection

Literacy Is  Powerful!

Pssst! We're Sharing Our Secrets!
Quick Tips: Homework HELP!

Is homework giving you a headache?
Want to go from "I'M DREADING THIS!" to "I'M DONE!"? Read on!

➤ Figure out the best time for your child to complete homework. Is it right after school or following dinner? Ideal times may vary from child to child. Experiment to see what works best. Consider other family commitments, too. Be sure it's not too late when homework gets started. Tired cowboys (or cowgirls) and homework don't mix!

➤ Once you settle on the best time, stick to the schedule.

➤ Turn off the TV and other distractions. Noise is a no-no.

➤ Begin with the toughest assignment first. Save easy—or favorite—for last. Just like dessert.

➤ Be available and willing to help, but don't do the work for your child. You already passed. Cheer your child on. He can pass, too!

➤ Stay positive. Don't yell or criticize. If you're losing your cool, walk away for a minute. None of us thrives on negative energy. Talk with the teacher if homework seems too tough or takes too long to complete.

➤ Take a break! Get up and stretch. Enjoy a light snack.

➤ Exchange jokes or tell a funny story about your day. Your child will get back to work recharged. And you will, too!

➤ Pat yourself on the back. You do a great job building important life skills when you make sure your child completes tasks. He (or she) did it! Yes!

Working Together to Strengthen Literacy and the Home–School Connection

Literacy  Is Powerful!

Pssst! We're Sharing Our Secrets!
Quick Tips:
Looking for a Good Book

Finding the right book at the right time keeps your child interested in reading. And that's a good thing! Kids who read do better in school, and kids who do better in school feel better about themselves and are more likely to succeed.

1. When looking for a good book for your child, consider his or her interests. What is your child curious about? What *does* your child like to do most? Does your child enjoy humor? Love mysteries? Is your child always ready for action and adventure? Nuts about animals? Crazy about science?

2. Next, visit the library or bookstore. Ask for help finding books that are just right for your child's interests and age.

3. Another way to pick great books is to look for award winners. Here are a few awards given to children's books. Happy Book Hunting!

- **Caldecott Medal:** *best picture books*
- **Newbery Medal:** *outstanding books for middle graders*
- **Pura Belpré Award:** *honors books about Latino culture by Latino authors and illustrators*
- **Coretta Scott King Awards:** *honors books by African American authors and illustrators*
- **Theodor Seuss Geisel Award:** *best books for beginning readers*
- **Sid Fleischman Humor Award:** *best funny books*
- **Robert F. Sibert Informational Book Award:** *best factual books*

Working Together to Strengthen Literacy and the Home–School Connection

Literacy Is  Powerful!

Pssst! We're Sharing Our Secrets!
Avoid the Summer Slide!
Strive for the Summer Rise!

Summer should be fun. It should be a stretch of time to relax, recharge, and play. Help your child discover the joy in reading by keeping it stress-free, relaxing, and rewarding. Your child will avoid the Summer Slide, trading up for the Summer Rise! Here's how to make it happen:

- We do what we love. We avoid what we don't. Nurture good feelings about reading:
  - Praise your child when he reads. Be specific. Point out something great going on. Example: "I heard you laughing when you read that book! What's so funny?" "I love to see you searching for the right book at the library. Did you see the one about...?"
  - Read with your child. Who doesn't love attention?
  - Make room for reading every day. Just like building muscle, the more time with a book, the stronger the reader!
  - For kids who won't read, link a book to something they're crazy about: soccer, horses, space, crafts, dinosaurs, or magic!
- Let your child choose the book. When kids pick books, they're more likely to finish them . . . and reach for another!
  - Don't worry about reading level. It's summer. Your child is reading and enjoying books. End of story.
  - Series, comics, re-reading old favorites—it's all good. It's time with a book . . . READING!

Working Together to Strengthen Literacy and the Home–School Connection

Literacy Is  Powerful!

Pssst! We're Sharing Our Secrets!
For Real?

Books filled with facts can be fascinating—especially when those facts are about something we're interested in. Snag your child's interest in reading with an informational or nonfiction book on a subject he or she cares about. It's like reeling in a hungry fish. For real!

Try this bait:

◊ **Steve Jenkins**—amazing animal facts! Grades 1–3
◊ **Magic School Bus** series—a mix of science & fantasy! Grades 2–3
◊ **Vicki Cobb and Gail Gibbons**—all sorts of science! Grades 1–3
◊ **Jon Scieszka**—wacky tales sneak in history, math, & science! Grades 3–5
◊ **Doreen Rappaport**—stunning biographies. Grades 1–4
◊ **Steve Sheinkin**—another stunner! Grades 5 and up
◊ **Greg Tang**—math fun in rhyme! Grades K–5
◊ **David A. Adler**—math facts. Grades 1–4
◊ **Kathleen Krull**—absolutely amazing, factual, and funny! Grades 3–6
◊ **Russell Freedman, Jim Murphy, Susan Campbell Bartoletti, Tanya Lee Stone, Candace Fleming**—award-winning nonfiction authors. Grades 4 and up

Note: Maturity, interests, and reading levels vary among children. Choose books accordingly.

Working Together to Strengthen Literacy and the Home–School Connection

Literacy Is  Powerful!

Pssst! We're Sharing Our Secrets!
Reading Doesn't Only Mean Books...

Reading takes place whenever we see print and make sense out of it. When we "get" what the words mean, that's called comprehension—a very long word, and a very important skill. We need to "get it" to learn. The more we read and understand, the more we "get."

Help kids "get it" everywhere they go. Here are a few ways to help your kid read and understand every day in all sorts of ways.

- Ask your child to read billboards to you as you drive around town. Cheer when younger kids read (but keep your hands on the wheel!). With older kids, discuss the message or what the advertiser is selling and how the billboard is trying to appeal to readers.
- Have your child read the TV listings to find favorite shows and times. Read the episode summaries, too!

- Ask your child to read a piece of mail to you while you fold laundry or unpack groceries.
- Have kiddos read cereal boxes, nutrition info, recipes, and soup cans for heating directions! Bake with your child. Read the whole recipe first and re-read the steps as needed. It's good practice (for reading and baking!).
- Ask your child to pick out a greeting card at the store the next time you need one—and not by the picture, but by the WORDS inside!
- Read magazines, newspapers, church and club news, and online information together.

Working Together to Strengthen Literacy and the Home–School Connection

Literacy Is Powerful!

Pssst! We're Sharing Our Secrets!
Try the 20-Minute Turn-Off!

Turn off the TV and other media, silence your cell phone, and
Turn to a book instead
Talk to your kids (and listen)
Toy time (Together)!
(Stop)Texting

Spending time talking, listening, and reading with your child lengthens attention span and builds listening, speaking, and reading skills. When you give your child your undivided attention you build self-esteem and the bonds between you. Your kid feels better about himself and his world when you

Take the Time.
It Makes a Difference.

Try the 20-Minute Turn-Off

And then make it a habit.
You'll be glad you did it for your kid—and yourself.

Working Together to Strengthen Literacy and the Home–School Connection

Literacy Is   Powerful!

Pssst! We're Sharing Our Secrets!
Terrific Titles!

Clueing You in to Mysteries that Make Readers of Kids

Kids love a mystery! Finding clues and figuring out "who dunnit" is appealing. Check one of these books out of the library and be prepared to yell, "Lights Out!" more than once. Because believe me, it's hard to stop turning the pages. Who did it? You'll have to read the book yourself to find out . . .

Grades K–2

Guess Again!, by Mac Barnett, illustrated by Adam Rex
Look Book, by Tana Hoban
The Mystery, by Maxwell Eaton III
The Pumpkin Mystery, by Carol Wallace, illustrated by Steve Björkman

Grades 3–5

Bunnicula series, by James Howe
Chomp, Flush, Hoot (and other books intended for children), by Carl Hiassen
Sammy Keyes series, by Wendelin Van Draanen
Books by Blue Balliett, Kate Messner, and Tony Abbott

Note: Maturity, interests, and reading levels vary among children. Choose books accordingly.

Working Together to Strengthen Literacy and the Home–School Connection

Literacy Is  Powerful!

Pssst! We're Sharing Our Secrets!
Terrific Titles!

We love our school families, and we think our young readers will love the families found in these stories! Here are great choices for reading aloud or for independent readers to pick up on their own. Tip: Occasionally, read aloud the first chapter of a book to your middle grader and then leave the book lying around! You may just snag a reader! Then find another book to read aloud . . .

Grades K–2
Old Bear and His Cub, by Olivier Dunrea
Grammy Lamby and the Secret Handshake, by Kate Klise and M. Sarah Klise
The Napping House, by Audrey Wood, illustrated by Don Wood
We're Going on a Bear Hunt, by Michael Rosen and Helen Oxenbury

Grades 3–5
The Brilliant Fall of Gianna Z., by Kate Messner
Esperanza Rising, by Pam Muñoz Ryan
Little House on the Prairie series, by Laura Ingalls Wilder
Walk Two Moons and *Granny Torelli Makes Soup*, by Sharon Creech
The Watsons Go to Birmingham—1963, by Christopher Paul Curtis

Note: Maturity, interests, and reading levels vary among children. Choose books accordingly.

Working Together to Strengthen Literacy and the Home–School Connection

Literacy Is  Powerful!

Pssst! We're Sharing Our Secrets!
Terrific Titles!

Who says books aren't fun? Here's a stack of interactive books for kids to enjoy! Let's get reading AND doing!

Primary Grades

Can You find It? series, published by the Metropolitan Museum of Art/Abrams

The Jolly Pocket Postman, by Janet and Allan Ahlberg

Walk This World: A Celebration of Life in a Day, by Lotta Nieminen

Middle Grades

Maps and Geography; U.S. Presidents, and other titles in the Ken Jennings's Junior Genius Guides series

Mythology, Dragonology, and other titles in the Ologies series, published by Candlewick

For All Ages

Pop-Up Books created by Robert Sabuda (various titles)

Discover More series (various informational titles for various ages), published by Scholastic

Note: Maturity, interests, and reading levels vary among children. Choose books accordingly.

Working Together to Strengthen Literacy and the Home–School Connection

Literacy Is   Powerful!

Appendix

Literacy Booster Event Attendance Register

Event:

Date:

Please PRINT your name and contact info.

1.

2.

3.

4.

5.

6.

7.

8.

9.

10.

11.

12.

13.

14.

15.

16.

17.

18.

19.

20.

21.

22.

23.

24.

25.

Thanks to all for attending this Literacy Booster Event!
~ Your Literacy Partners ~

Sometimes people forget how big everything was when they were little...

—Children's author, Mercer Mayer

Literacy Booster Event Evaluation Forms

Literacy Booster Event Evaluation

1. Please rate this Literacy Booster Event:

   Excellent   Very Good   Average   Poor

2. What did you find most helpful about this event?

3. Is there anything you feel could be improved?

4. Do you have suggestions for topics for future Literacy Booster Events?

5. Suggestions/Overall Comments (continue on the back if necessary).

Literacy Booster Event Evaluation

1. Please rate this Literacy Booster Event:

   Excellent   Very Good   Average   Poor

2. What did you find most helpful about this event?

3. Is there anything you feel could be improved?

4. Do you have suggestions for topics for future Literacy Booster Events?

5. Suggestions/Overall Comments (continue on the back if necessary).

Literacy Booster
Meeting Notes

The following ideas were shared by parents/caregivers who attended our

recent meeting, "_____,"

held on _____.

Thanks to all for attending this Literacy Booster Event!
~ Your Literacy Partners ~

Sometimes people forget how big everything was when they were little...

—*Children's author, Mercer Mayer*